FOR

Solitude

Solitude

Recovering the power of alone

Simon Parke

Solitude

Published and printed in the United States of America and the United Kingdom
by White Crow Books; an imprint of White Crow Productions Ltd.

For information, contact White Crow Books
at P. O. Box 1013 Guildford, GU1 9EJ United Kingdom,
or e-mail to info@whitecrowbooks.com.

Cover Designed by Butterflyeffect
Interior production by essentialworks.co.uk
Interior design by Perseus Design

Paperback ISBN 978-1-907661-96-9
eBook ISBN 978-1-907661-97-6

Non Fiction / Body, Mind & Spirit / Parapsychology

Published by White Crow Books

www.whitecrowbooks.com

Acknowledgements

This book has emerged from an intense two months of writing over the summer of 2011. I have never completed a manuscript in such a short time nor been so unsure in the act of creation. So friends along the way have been important. After all, every act of creation is the act of a community.

So I am very grateful to my web friends with whom I shared the idea at the outset. You have been most kind, encouraging and insightful, the best sort of community.

And thank you Shellie for reading the third draft of the book and finding something there. I was wilting at that stage but you gave me strength to cry 'On, On!' and to complete four further drafts.

My thanks also to Harry for his beautiful and sensitive picture which is the cover of the book. Portraying the path of solitude, it is the essence of the book in picture form.

And my final thanks are to Jon, my publisher at Whitecrow, for running with this idea and generally, for providing a home for some books I'm very proud of. We always talk about 'getting lucky' with a book one day. That would be nice, but we both well know we're pretty lucky now.

I dedicate this book to the mountain.

Man cannot long survive without air, water
and sleep. Next in importance comes food.
And close on it's heals, solitude.

Thomas Szasz

Contents

Reader's Notes

I write of solitude amid the sound of breaking glass, roaring flames and angry shouts. Am I wasting my time?

It's been an extraordinary week of violence and looting in England. For a few mad days, the social fabric of many of our cities has been ripped apart by aggression, mob power, opportunism and fear. It all started at the bottom of my road in North London.

Opinion columns have been eager to offer activist solutions with lists of things we must do. Yet perhaps an absence of doing would be more creative. As Blaise Pascal observed, 'All men's miseries derive from not being able to sit quietly in a room alone.' Could that be true? Might the answer lie in learning to be still?

As smoke billows into the air and people cry out for answers, I have never been more convinced of the human need for solitude or for the nation's need to recover the power of alone.

These days will pass but others will come. Personally and nationally, we will again stand frightened and amazed at what we and other people do.

But this is the truth: at the heart of our actions tomorrow is the quality of our solitude today.

If we wish to learn how to live, we must first learn how to be still.

*

This book is written to help you onto the path of solitude - often an abandoned way and one overgrown with distraction, ignorance and fear.

It is a slow book. It's written for your consideration rather than your rush; sprint through and you will miss the point. If you like to rush, read it through once to see what it is and then relax, slow down and read it again; like a fine wine, it will be better with age. To help you slow down, asterisks appear in the text, like a lay-by on the road. You don't have to stop, you can always drive on - but they're a place to pause and eat sandwiches if you wish.

There is an order to the chapters early on. If solitude is new or perhaps frightening for you then the first ten chapters may help to settle and guide you. They introduce the subject and the practice and provide a foundation for what follows.

Techniques for solitude can help and they do appear along the way. But more important than technique is understanding, without which technique becomes dry. If we understand why we're doing something, the 'how's' will begin to take care of themselves. Wherever you're starting from, I hope this book will help you into a profounder understanding of solitude.

The book has a Q&A feel to it as I've allowed my alter-ego to appear in the text. His questions and comments are in italics and I hope you enjoy the conversation. In my experience, the question and answer session after the talk is often more revealing than the talk itself.

And at the back of the book is a brief biography of everyone I quote, just in case you wonder who is saying these things. They're a fascinating bunch of people, some of whom you may wish to get to know better. But remember always this is your story and not theirs.

*

I must keep you from the path no longer, so I now stop my chatter and wish you well.

We shall learn again to be still, as once we were in the womb; we shall recover the power of alone.

August 2011
www.simonparke.com

1. Starting out

How do you feel about solitude?

Solitude is the active path towards inner silence.

That's your definition of it?

It is, yes. It reconnects us to our inner knowing which is not the same as our outer knowing.

So why do we find it so hard?

That's a good question.

I won't be fobbed off with compliments.

There'll be precious few of those, I promise. But bear with me and we'll discover answers worthy of eternity.

Answers worthy of tomorrow will do me.

Fair point – we musn't get too flighty. So let's start with a quotation.

I hope we'll hear from a good spread of people.

We will, my friend, and they're all different. But I should say at the outset that I'm not concerned with their various labels; just grateful for their truth. And remember, everyone quoted has a brief biography at the back of the book.

Noted.

So here are some words from Sister Wendy Beckett. You may have seen her on television talking about art but she spends most of her time alone:

'The capacity for silence – a deep creative awareness of one's inner truth – is what distinguishes us as humans.'

What do you reckon?

That's a noble way to start.

It's good to be reminded of our nobility at the outset; we are noble people with untold capacity for understanding.

And when put like that, who wouldn't want silence?

I agree. Who on earth doesn't desire a deep creative awareness of their inner truth? There's only one response, surely: 'Let us please be silent!'

But it doesn't work like that?

No, it doesn't because for many humans, solitude is a vision of terror, something to flee and fear.

Why so?

The path of solitude presents difficulties because to walk it, we must leave things behind.

What sort of things?

All sorts of things. It asks us to leave behind much that seems to define our lives like friends, work, mobiles, internet, our plans and other distractions with which we fill our days.

I can see that does sound a bit threatening.

'If I leave those behind,' people say, 'what on earth will I do? It's like jumping into a void.'

I'm feeling uneasy already.

It's good to notice our reactions at the outset. Truthful noticing will be important as we walk, so we start now. Allow your breathing to settle and consider this: how do you feel about solitude? And how do you feel about silence?

Honestly?

Only honest answers allowed.

*

Whatever your feelings about these things - and there must be the spark of desire in you to have got this far - it's my happy task in this book to describe and commend solitude to you.

I'm listening.

And whether a beginner or old hand, I believe we're always learning to be still, always starting out and always facing difficulty.

There are no experts?

An expert is just someone who has started again often.

I can foresee difficulties as we set out. Are you going to help?

I hope so. In the pages ahead you'll find small bridges across the waters of difficulty.

And where do the bridges take us?

To the space beyond where the air is clear and the views good. There we find our sky nature, that other nature which we've forgotten or maybe repressed.

My sky nature?

It's what the Tibetans call it, though you can call it what you will. We won't get hung up on words. But the meaning of our life can grow small and pale amid the stresses and strains of life.

Tell me about it! I often wonder what I'm doing with my days.

In solitude there is an expansion of what it means to be alive; we are closer to the blue sky.

So let the journey begin.

That's the spirit. But be steady rather than frantic; steady lasts longer and gets further.

Is there anything else to remember?

Remember your nobility, walk at your own pace, rest when you need to but keep your eyes set on the destination. Solitude is not about our speed through the forest but about our direction.

And that is?

Daily, we set our compass towards the clearing that is inner silence. We don't always get there; but that clearing is our aim.

2. Stepping off the beaten track

Do you find it easy to stop what you're doing?

To find solitude, we have to stop what we're doing and this is not easy.

That's true. It's hard getting off the treadmill of familiar activity.

There's a voice of panic inside us: 'Stop what I'm doing? Never! What I'm doing has kept me me happily distracted for years! Why stop now? Better the devil you know!'

Or perhaps we believe that what we're doing is really crucial.

True. We might feel that our work is simply too important to stop. That's another voice inside us: 'I'm a person of action. I get things done! I'm no navel-gazing day dreamer!'

Don't get me going on day dreamers - I can't abide them.

I note your opinion. But I've always felt that if something is worth doing, it's also worth not doing. Does that make sense?

Not really.

However important our tasks, we're all the better for putting them down occasionally. If we learn to stop what we're doing – even if it's wonderful work - we return to it in much better shape: less pompous, refreshed and more clearer-sighted.

So more effective?

No offence but yes. It's dull people who tell you how busy they are, for busyness is all that holds them together. It's their particular drug. So here's the question: is stopping difficult for you?

Honestly?

Honestly.

Sometimes stopping feels like dying. And as you say, it's because of what I must leave behind.

Your honesty does you credit and will help your walk no end. But although stopping is hard, it's necessary.

Convince me. I've always regarded it as something of an indulgence.

The fact is, whatever spiritual, religious or intellectual veneer you give yourself, you are your psychology - so it is worth pausing to give it some attention.

Hang on a second. How do you mean, 'You are your psychology'?

Your psychology is the puppet master and you are the puppet; you do as it says. Even your spirituality does what your psychology says. That's why it's important to look after your psychology.

I didn't expect to hear that when I got up this morning. I'm to look after my psychology?

Look after your psychology and your psychology will look after you. And you do this both for your sake and the sake of those who must endure you day by day.

I see. I always thought I was pretty straight forward.

Straight forward? You're as straight forward as a corkscrew.

I'm not sure that's very polite.

6

I'm not interested in being polite. I'm interested in your life and in you exploring life. I'm ambitious for you and the deep creative awareness of inner silence is your friend.

Why?

It makes the world a better place for you and everyone else. Without such awareness our actions become blind, lazy, mechanical and self-serving.

And we begin this change by stopping?

Yes, we learn to be still; we allow ourselves to stop. If something is worth doing, it's worth not doing.

*

This chapter's called 'Stepping off the beaten track'. Why?

It's what we do in solitude, because it is not a well-travelled way. In solitude, we step off the beaten track of our life, away from the joggers in our mind and the street lights of popular assumption.

I like those word pictures.

Instead, we choose the narrow path of withdrawal, walk through the rough space of our forgotten selves and find a place to sit in the deep caverns of our existence where no one can watch us and no one else may come. Does that sound mad?

No, it sounds rather romantic.

Well, it is a love story in a way, a passion for life, people and truth.

And it's a passion that takes us great distances?

In a way it does, but in another way, it's simply a coming home to ourselves. In solitude, we can gather ourselves and become people again.

Aren't we always people?

We might imagine we're always people but this is not so. Very often, we become machines, reacting in automatic fashion to a life we're barely aware of.

Solitude comes to us quietly and gently wakes us up to ourselves and the world.

*

So where will solitude take me?

I've described solitude as the active path towards inner silence; this gets to the heart of the matter. But how far we travel the path on any given occasion will vary. It's our intentions, not our achievement, which colour our world.

I like quiet places sometimes.

That's good because those will help. But outer stillness is not the same as inner stillness.

No?

Sometimes, despite our tranquil surroundings, we may feel there's so much inner noise we've reached everything but silence.

That's true. Yesterday there was a situation that I just couldn't get out of my mind.

This is OK; it is what it is.

Yes, but I wish it wasn't!

So you're not as you wish to be?

Of course I'm not.

Well, don't judge yourself or your predicament too harshly. That's self-indulgence. We simply note the noise, whatever form it takes and turn it into a companion on our journey.

How?

We say something like: 'Hello, inner noise. How are you? You seem very noisy today, denying me any silence. But it's time for you to go now, when you're ready. You are not who I am and these days, I'm looking beyond you.'

And we find help along the way. If our heart is set on solitude, we find that the world around us is full of prompts and guides. It's almost falling over itself to help us.

Really?

Whether it's a cloud in the sky, a ten minute train delay or a sudden and unexpected opportunity, creation conspires to help us on our way, to bring us to the healing pool of inner silence. Creation is a great friend of ours.

It's strange to imagine myself friends with creation.

Then do get used to it because it's a truth for all seasons.

❋

So there's endless help on the journey?

There is, yes. But in the end, the journey will be yours alone. There's no second-hand solitude, no borrowed solitude and no one can lend you some of theirs. The power of alone will be your discovery and it's a power that looks like clarity, compassion, courage, spontaneity and hope.

That doesn't sound much like me.

It doesn't? Then you don't know yourself. Listen to Hafiz, who always hits the nail on the head:

'I wish I could show you, when you are lonely or in darkness, the astonishing light of your own being.'

I'll have to take that on trust. But let's be practical for a moment: give me some tips.

Experts only become experts by experimenting and this is what we'll do as we learn to be still.

'More than anything else, experiment with solitude,' writes Julia Cameron. 'You will need to make a commitment to quiet time. Try to acquire the habit of checking in with your self. Several times a day, just take a beat and ask yourself how you are feeling. Listen to your answer. Respond kindly.'

Hopefully this book will become a series of small experiments. Pick it up when you need help; put it down when the words have done their work and are getting in the way.

Your inner journey is a great deal more important than the next paragraph.

So how are you feeling?

3. The purpose of solitude

Will solitude keep us sane?

In 1988, the psychiatrist Anthony Storr published a book called *Solitude*.

Why?

His main argument was that solitary pursuits 'play a greater part in the economy of human happiness than modern psychoanalysts and their followers allow'.

What was the reaction?

The book made waves at the time, as it went against popular assumptions. Traditionally, psychoanalysis had viewed those with a preference for solitude as deficient in some way and in need of help. It was known that certain psychological conditions such as schizophrenia and the schizoid personality disorder were strongly linked to a tendency to seek solitude. So solitude was regarded as the refuge of the insane or the inadequate.

That's not a great sales pitch for the practice.

And taking the lead from psychoanalysis, society adopted this assumption and continues to do so today. A host of self-help books, women's magazines and dating sites extol interpersonal relationships as life's Holy Grail.

It's what people want to read about.

So there's advice about finding relationships, starting relationships, improving relationships and leaving relationships - but no advice about the joys of solitude. The message is clear.

And what's that?

Our lives are to be defined by others rather than ourselves. 'How am I?' and 'How is my love life?' almost become the same question.

I suppose there is an element of that.

People sometimes come to me to reflect on their lives. When speaking with them, I often find myself saying: 'You seem to be allowing your life to be defined by other people.'

It's the spirit of the age.

It's the spirit of a mad age - an age frightened or ignorant of solitude.

But you say Storr's book had other ideas?

Certainly. Instead of seeing solitude as strange, he highlighted the creativity and emotional maturity that could be found there. His book was ground-breaking in psychiatric circles and proved reassuring for many whose love of solitude had previously felt odd and out of step with everyone else.

Solitude was allowed once again!

But although the book was startling and refreshing in its time, it said only what the great religions and philosophers had been saying for hundreds if not thousands of years. After all, it was 6000 years ago that Buddha said:

'Each of you must make himself his island; make himself and no one else his refuge.'

It's a truth that keeps getting lost in the rush for relationship.

So is this book a repeat of Storr's book?

No, the two are different. Anthony Storr's focus is on the use of solitude by brilliant scientists, philosophers and composers like Descartes, Newton, Beethoven, Kafka and Wittgenstein. Intense creativity demanded intense solitude.

And this book?

I'm a bit more democratic. The claim here is that solitude is essential for everyone. It's a healing place, a renewing place, a deepening place crucial to mental and spiritual health, whether we're a bus driver, a doctor or a latter-day Van Gogh.

We're all creating a life from the raw material inside us.

Very good. And the life we create is the shape of our solitude.

So a question for you: if the human alone is the human, what sort of human are you?

∗

So to clarify: what is solitude?

Solitude is the active walk into inner silence.

Where do we start from?

Wherever we happen to be.

The journey may begin with others and amid noise. But with the decision taken, we leave others and the noise to themselves and enter an increasing degree of silence. It may be for ten minutes, an hour, a week or a life time; the time doesn't matter because the only moment is now. It's about the intent, about the desire to approach the creative awareness of silence.

And it's not just a matter of leaving behind external things?

That's right. We all know that leaving a party does not always mean leaving the people at the party. They can continue to inhabit our heads and hearts long after we've physically left them. Indeed, the inner noise of feelings and thoughts is sometimes all the noisier in silence.

I think that's why one of my friends has to go to sleep with music playing. He doesn't like the things which fill the silence.

Ah, the mental ghosts. In the practice of solitude, we learn to leave inner things behind like these mental ghosts.

Mental ghosts - what are they?

They're the feelings that inhabit the hurt of our childhood and return again and again in adult life.

That's a big thought.

It's a true thought. But these ghosts have been spoiled and indulged for too long. Their day is done. The search now is for a place apart which frees us to enjoy the world rather than being crippled by it.

I'd like to enjoy the world.

Good. So we seek within ourselves a clear space, a place that is simple, calm and honouring and which offers a sense of value and balance in our lives. Some people call this place 'God' and as we've heard, Buddha called it a refuge.

Does it matter what name we give this place?

The name we give it is less important than the experience we have. Increasingly, we find a place we can call our own.

You could go there now.

4. Fear of solitude

What if solitude frightens me?

Albert Einstein once said: 'I live in that solitude which is painful in youth, but delicious in the years of maturity.'

So he got there in the end, but he had problems early on. Can you understand that?

I take the fear of solitude very seriously. I've seen it in the faces of people when they hear I'm working on this book and not just in the faces of the young.

Is this fear something new?

I don't think so. 'Solitude is the mother of anxieties,' said Publilius Syrus in the 1st century BC so clearly it's been around for a while.

As far as I'm concerned, fear of solitude is quite understandable.

I agree. It's a path that leads us away from what Henri Nouwen calls 'the scaffolding of our daily life' and for many this is a horrific thought.

Without that scaffolding, we imagine our house will collapse.

That's the fear and our scaffolding, of course, is our dependence addictions.

Dependence addictions?

These addictions will differ but they're the things that give meaning to our day and without which we become twitchily restless.

Why are you looking at me?

For some it's cocaine, for some their iPad and for others it's their social diary. I remember a woman who would panic if she had a spare evening in the week, in which she didn't have a social activity pencilled in.

I'm too busy working to have an addiction.

Maybe. Or maybe work is your addiction. Perhaps you keep busy because you fear the alternative. Our addictions are sometimes the thing we complain about the most. Yet if they were taken away we'd feel lost.

I take your point. I know a mum who's always complaining about how tiring it is being a mother. But I reckon she needs her child more than the child needs her. It's the ultimate displacement activity.

We're all experts at filling our time because we fear the consequences of not filling it. Perhaps that mum avoids solitude because she's afraid of being bored, being empty or being exposed.

Or all three.

So you can see why she runs from it. People imagine the house of their life is a fragile affair and might collapse without the scaffolding of distraction.

It's a voice of panic inside: 'What am I and who am I if my daily networks and rat-runs are taken from me?'

That sort of thing, yes and it's a real terror. Some would prefer to meet their worst enemy in the street rather than dismantle the scaffolding and seek out their hearts in the silence.

*

The terror is real enough – so what do we do with it?

We understand it but we don't bow to it. Terror likes us to grovel and comply with its desolate demands but why give it the pleasure? The truth of the matter – which your terror obscures – is this: it's not solitude we need fear but the absence of solitude.

We are to fear the absence of solitude?

Of course! Be terrified of a life devoid of stillness and reflection because the damage you do to yourself and others will be significant.

That's a new way to look at it.

✳

I'm reminded of the story told by Carl Jung about the priest who came to see him. He felt the power was going out of his ministry. Do you know this anecdote?

I'm not sure. Start and I'll tell you.

Well, Jung recommended that he spend one evening a week by himself. The priest agreed to this plan and left.

When he returned the following week, Jung asked him how his evening alone had gone. The priest said it went fine. He'd watched TV and enjoyed it.

Yes, I do know this story.

Well, you'll learn more hearing it a second time; you'll catch the second truth.

OK.

So Jung then pointed out to the priest that he was meant to spend the evening alone, without the TV for company. He encouraged him to try the same thing again the next week. The priest agreed and left.

When he returned the following week, Jung asked him how it had gone. The priest said it went fine. He'd read a book all evening and enjoyed it. Jung pointed out that the he was meant to spend the evening alone, without the company of a book.

The priest became exasperated. How could he possibly spend the evening just with himself?

'Well, if you don't want to spend time with yourself,' observed Jung, 'are you surprised that others don't wish to spend time with you?'

It's a good story.

It's good because the priest sounds very similar to you and I. But whatever fear holds us back from the path of solitude, it has no more authority than the slight chill of a turquoise sea on a hot day. I feel the chill, ignore it, take the plunge and delight in the water. Silence will never betray us.

※

We started with Roman words and we close with some more. These are spoken by Epictetus in his *Discourses*. They're words of encouragement to frightened adventurers in solitude:

'When you close your doors and make darkness within, remember to never say that you are alone, for you are not alone; nay, God is within you and your genius is within. And what need have they of light to see what you are doing?'

The path is yours and safer than you imagine.

5. Learning solitude

Is it time to make sense of your life?

I've been asking around about solitude.

Any discoveries?

Most people thought it was a bad word, a word they were uneasy with.

I'm not surprised. Wikipedia links it to bad relationships, infectious diseases and mental disorder in the first sentence of their description. It doesn't encourage you to pursue the matter.

And then how about this response from one woman: 'How on earth can someone like me learn solitude? I'm 43, a keen follower of a wide variety of distractions – and it's not like there are night classes or anything!'

Well, there's wisdom there.

There is?

She's at least seen that solitude is something which must be learned.

Learned?

For many of us, solitude will have to be learned because we didn't learn it as children. We learned many things when young but not how to be happily still.

I remember being told to 'Shut up!' all the time but I suppose that's different.

Certainly we didn't experience the education described here by the Indian Standing Bear:

'Training began with children, who were taught to sit still and enjoy it. They were taught to use their organs of smell, to look where there was apparently nothing to see and to listen intently when all seemingly was quiet.'

No, that wasn't my home.

And he concludes with this line: 'A child who cannot sit still is a half-developed child.'

So presumably an adult who cannot sit still is a half-developed adult?

*

Maybe if I'd learned it as a child, it would all be simple. As it is, solitude feels rather complicated.

There's nothing complicated about solitude. Just think of it as two steps.

And they are?

First there is the physical withdrawal from the world. This can pose problems, but may prove the easy part. Here we remove ourselves from the outer distractions of life – people, mobiles, screens, interruption, clocks.

OK. I'd put that under the 'Simple but Demanding' heading.

Second, we remove ourselves from our inner distractions, lived out in our racing and unruly mind.

And how on earth do we do that?

The best way to start is with a growing awareness of our breathing.

What does that achieve?

It stills and simplifies our lives. As we focus on our breathing, thoughts come and then go. We notice them but we do not follow them. They want us to play chase but we refuse; instead, we return to our breathing.

What's in our breathing?

The present, untouched by our mind. In fact, why not do this now for two minutes, wherever you are? It's a revolution of the spirit, every time it's attempted.

What - just listen to my breathing?

❋

Solitude is more about saying 'no' than saying 'yes'.

How do you mean?

Perhaps you're waiting to see the doctor. You could pick up one of the magazines available. But if you said 'no' to the magazine, you could listen instead to your breathing, gather yourself and become aware of the moment.

I suppose so.

Or perhaps you're waiting at the bus stop. You could text someone. But if you said 'no' to the text, you could focus instead on some aspect of the scenery around you – a tree, a window, an old door – and allow it to become a meditation. You look at your chosen object, note it well and allow creation to speak.

Because creation is my friend.

Well remembered.

I do my best.

Or perhaps you're waiting in a supermarket queue. You could spend your time getting frustrated, expressed in a tense body and hateful thoughts towards those ahead of you and the cashier. But if you said 'no' to all that, and accepted your circumstances, you could become conscious for the first time in the day. You may have been living on automatic up until that moment. Then a simple 'no' opens the door of awareness.

In each of these instances, you chose an active walk into inner silence.

I wasn't expecting solitude in the supermarket.

They may only be brief experiences but sometimes solitude is brief. It's the habit that matters not the length of each stay. Different days offer different possibilities.

We start off by carving solitude out of our day, until in time, we find ourselves carving our day out of our solitude.

*

Can others help us to be solitary?

Of course. Those Indian children had teachers to lead them into stillness and perhaps we have a yoga class or meditation group. When I was a priest, the evening service was sometimes a half hour of silence – no words at all. There is something very strong in doing silence together as football crowds know.

I think some relationships I have make me feel still inside, others less so.

That's good to notice. But we'll need to develop our own resources, for ultimately we must be caretakers of our solitude; we cannot depend on others. We can thank them for their help and then leave them behind.

That sounds a bit savage.

Removing a cancerous growth is savage but most people would call it kind savagery.

OK.

What may surprise us as we learn to say 'no' to distraction and 'yes' to solitude are the resources available within us.

I'm hoping that's true.

Hafiz reminded us earlier about the 'astonishing light' in our being which can still surprise us. And seven centuries later, a friend of mine recounted this story:

'Recently I had the opportunity to house sit for a friend, which enabled me to spend time alone.

As I share a home with two grown up daughters and a grandchild and I also work in a happy but often busy nursery school environment, time alone is not something that I am used to getting. It is far more normal for me to be fighting for quiet moments.

But being given this space really was a beautiful gift and as I felt myself relax and settle into a new routine, I began to notice and become aware of things that were happening inside.

On the evenings that I visited my own home to pick up things, I noticed that I was eager to get back to the uncluttered space of my friend's house. I found that I wanted to spend time alone and this is not something that I was consciously aware of before. I knew it was good for me to spend time alone, but I didn't know it was something I actually wanted.'

That's interesting. I can see we're poorly educated in solitude and that as with your friend, life has to step in to help us.

We're taught as children to take external life seriously but not our inner life; this is what it is to be the walking unconscious.

You mean we're taught as children to become unconscious?

Precisely.

Which leaves us frightened of solitude.

But saying goodbye to that fear opens all sorts of doors. My friend continues: 'As I become more aware of enjoying this time alone, I realise I am no longer frightened of my own company and that I am willing to receive anything that arises. I may not always like it, but I am willing to receive it.'

∗

In a way, it's like learning a new language; a new language of life.

Or at least putting punctuation into our language of life; punctuation which makes everything make sense. A paragraph without punctuation is a mess and that is true of many people's lives.

Punctuation was never my strong point.

That's OK. We begin to learn today and then begin again tomorrow and begin again the next day. The truly wise are eternal beginners.

That's reassuring.

And as we begin each day, we find ourselves astonished by the help creation offers and warmed by how familiar and homely it all feels. We leave others behind for a while and it's all right; we're strong enough.

So it's my life?

It is your life. As Storr says, 'In the end, one has to make sense of one's own life, however influential guidance from mentors may have been.'

It's time to take your leave. The unconscious child is waking up.

6. Withdrawal

Is it hard to leave others behind?

I've been searching for helpful quotes.

You'll be asking me to pay you next. So what did you find?

It's from Peter Hoeg: 'Never do I close my door behind me without being conscious that I am carrying out an act of charity towards myself.'

I like that.

Why?

I find it helpful. Withdrawal is essential for solitude and it isn't solitude until we have left everything behind. But we remember this: however challenging it may seem, it's an act of charity towards our selves.

So give generously?

Indeed.

But it's difficult. I'm a car with one gear and it's hard to change.

It's good to acknowledge the difficulties, because you can't say goodbye to something until you've said hello to it. Name the difficulties, it's the first step. But of course you have many more gears than one.

You think so?

I know so. But I don't deny that adjusting from one way of being to another way of being can be hard. A surprising number of soldiers found it difficult when the 2nd World War ended.

Really?

Yes, everyone expected them to be delighted when they put their guns down and returned to peacetime Britain. Yet beyond the bunting and the 'Welcome home' parties, many pined for the straight forward life they'd known in the armed forces and felt out of place in this new and uncertain environment. In the forces they'd obeyed commands; back home, they had to make the decisions for themselves. Adjusting was hard.

I can see the issues.

Neither is it by chance that most family rows are said to start within 15 minutes of people returning home after the day spent away. We go from one role and set of demands to another role and set of demands and the adjustments, like rocks falling on our path, can make us trip and stumble.

So we won't always skip merrily onto the path of solitude?

No, it's an adjustment and we'll need determination. But Anne Morrow Lindbergh puts steel in our resolve:

'We seem to be so frightened today of being alone that we never let it happen. Even if family and friends should fail, there is still the radio or television to fill the void...we can do our house work with soap opera heroes at our side...We choke the space with continuous music, chatter and companionship to which we do not even listen. It is simply there to fill the vacuum. When the noise stops there is no inner music to take its place. We must relearn to be alone.'

*

I'm wondering why she used the word 'relearn'. Is this something that we once had but have lost?

I think it is. I sense the world has taught us to have increasing problems with silence.

You often imply that we've lost much that we possessed as children. The popular assumption is that we start off in life not being very good at things and then gradually we get better. But you're saying the opposite?

In many areas of life, yes I am.

You're a bit of a lone voice there, I think.

Far from it. You may know of the recent test for divergent thinking in young people?

I'm not sure I do.

Divergent thinking is the ability to come up with different solutions given a situation. It's awareness that there's not one answer but many answers and is at the root of much creativity.

And you're telling me this because?

The test followed the same children as they grew up and the results are interesting. They were first conducted at kindergarten age where 98% of the children were rated at 'genius' level. The test was done again when the children were 10, by which time that figure was down to 50%.

Really?

By the time they were 15, it was considerably lower again.

Now, be honest – you might reasonably have expected it to be the other way round?

I might, yes.

Yet in this genuinely creative area, we discover that humans, exposed to a particular way of teaching and understanding as they grow up, actually go backwards; they become lesser people.

Disturbing.

And I have no doubt it's exactly the same in our relationship to solitude and silence. We do not start off life finding it hard and then get better. Rather, we start life finding it easy but lose this capacity along the way, to the extent that some find it almost impossible.

I think Lindburgh is right to speak of us relearning to be alone. And suddenly we better understand Jesus' call for us to become 'as children'.

*

So we're to relearn to be alone.

That's what we're doing yes, because solitude is an act of charity towards ourselves and therefore the world.

The world? What's the world got to do with it?

If we are psychologically healthy then our work is healthy and the world benefits. Withdrawing from the world is important if we wish to be a creative part of it; an inability to withdraw from the world reveals only that we're part of the problem.

We become saviours who are sicker than those we are trying to save?

Quite possibly, so we'll be aware of the need for self-discipline. Jesus, for instance, took himself off into the hills early in the morning, leaving his followers behind.

Despite his busy and demanding life?

No, *because* of his busy and demanding life. He wished to stay healthy rather than join the sick.

So how did he find the time?

We all make time for what we want to do. His followers would sometimes chase after him, puzzled by his actions. But Jesus knew that if something is worth doing – like carpentry, teaching and healing – it's also worth not doing. His followers just assumed you must be doing it all the time.

*

And some take the solitude thing a bit further.

I know you're interested in the 4th century Desert Fathers who decided on a most extreme form of withdrawal.

They do intrigue me.

We'll come back to them.

But why did they act as they did?

They left the cities of Asia Minor and travelled deep into the deserts of Egypt for no other reason than to be themselves.

Meaning?

They wished to be themselves as opposed to being someone else. They believed the world around them divided their wills and their lives and led them away from seeking the things that mattered.

They'd lost sight of themselves amid the distractions of the world?

That's right. Love them or hate them, they sought solitude to offset the corrosive and splintering power of the world. The goal of their solitude was purity of heart from which to see their true state, apart from the toxic influence of the culture of the day.

I hate deserts. I like mountains but not deserts.

We may not opt for the desert but the principle remains the same.

Even on a train journey?

A train journey? Well, why not? If we put down our book or switch off our music and seize a moment of solitude on the train, we enter the desert. In solitude I say goodbye to the outer voices that give me a phoney sense of well-being.

There are a lot of those.

There are, yes. They might be the real voices of friends or work colleagues. Or perhaps they're virtual voices, tweeting me reassurance that I'm alive in some way.

In solitude I say goodbye to these voices, which tug and pull at my ego, splintering unity within. Instead, I trust myself to my inner voice.

I'm not sure I'd recognise that.

Well, it won't be a strong voice at first; after all, it's not used to being listened to. But we're relearning, are we not? Each day, we learn.

Yes. I just didn't realise I'd lost so much along the way.

So listen now for the voice, your inner voice. Can you hear anything?

7. Acceptance

Is pretence killing your solitude?

I've been doing more research.

I'm impressed.

Here's another interesting response to solitude: 'There are too many buried bodies in my life. That's why I keep things busy. You can call it evasion if you like, but why give space to the unacceptable?'

There's definitely insight there.

It just sounds negative to me.

It is negative but it's naming an important truth.

Which is?

If we attempt solitude whilst evading something in our lives, then our solitude will be diminished.

What sort of things do people avoid?

It's a long list but might include death, fury, despair, sadness, shame, fear or other feelings or memories we reckon unacceptable.

Avoiding those things sounds eminently sensible to me.

Then we must agree to differ. Pretence kills more people than cancer and certainly hurts solitude.

Controversial.

It's only controversial in a mad world. In a sane world, it's quite obvious that pretence kills and we know it from our daily conversations with people.

How do you mean?

It is, for instance, an unsatisfying experience to speak with someone who for whatever reason cannot face certain topics. You sense them closing down when dangerous territory is neared or reached.

Yes, that's no fun.

It's like trying to go for a walk and constantly having your way barred. They are frightened people, threatened people and any exchange must be on their terms and within their narrow band of reality.

I agree, that is unsatisfying.

And the thing is - it's quite possible we treat ourselves in the same way.

How?

We may approach solitude willing to face certain aspects of our existence but determined to resist or ignore others. In doing so, we cut ourselves off from the magnificent grace of the honest moment.

The magnificent grace of the honest moment? Are you just back from poetry school?

I wish. But today it's worth considering whether there's anything you're unhappy with at present; anything you're fighting, resisting or angry about.

Is there any aspect of your life which is a no-go area at present? Is there something uncomfortable you do not want others to raise and do not wish to contemplate yourself?

I'll need time to consider that.

Then take the time.

*

We remember, however, that such things are quite normal so we won't punish ourselves over them. We're fragile people used to putting survival ahead of life.

I'm beginning to believe that's true.

We do no more than notice these things; we notice their dark shapes dancing in and out of view.

And then?

And then we breathe acceptance into our situation. Just for a moment, we allow what is; we allow things to be just the way they are. We allow ourselves our past and we allow ourselves our present.

I'm not sure I can do that.

In short, we put down our constant fight with reality. So much of our suffering arises from us trying to control what we cannot control. So instead, we step into the spacious halls of acceptance. Our body and spirit long for this experience; it's our mind which must put down the fight.

*

Joel S. Goldsmith was saying something similar when he wrote this:

'If we can sit perfectly quiet and perfectly still with no attempt to overcome, destroy, remove or escape from any situation or condition, the flow of the spirit will rush in and there will be freedom.'

There's a sense of impossibility about such an attitude.

I agree. Yet also present is a sense of truth. The invitation is to trust the path you walk if the journey made sense at the start.

Is that capacity for acceptance something we can always know?

The capacity for acceptance comes and goes within us. Its presence depends both on our circumstances and our past.

What's our past got to do with it?

Usually a great deal. Many of us emerged from childhood believing a very destructive lie.

What lie?

The lie was this: you are not good enough, you are not acceptable as you are.

And why is that such a dangerous lie? It seems a self-evident truth to me.

So you believed it then and still believe it now. But beware of this belief that was put inside you.

Why?

It is a lie leads us into all sorts of negativity as adults, both towards ourselves and the world. It makes it impossible to accept the present because it's impossible to accept ourselves.

I suppose it does.

So we notice when the lie appears within us but we do not now believe it. We let it go. Instead we remember that this moment is acceptable and we are acceptable. We relearn the truth that we are good enough; you relearn that you are good enough.

Are you saying I'm perfect?!

No, like everyone else, your beautiful statue is covered in weeds but that's not the point. Right now, at this very moment, you are good enough and in that sense you're quite perfect for now.

*

That's a peaceful place if you can get there.

We reach this place via acceptance and when we are healthy within, we have strength for this acceptance.

And when we're stressed?

When stressed, we have almost no capacity for it at all. But in solitude we dismantle stress. In solitude, a growing acceptance of our selves and the world is nurtured. Here the mind's restless memories and resistance are stilled. We become stressed less often.

You believe I can flourish?

A different future depends on a different present. You could start by accepting yourself and this moment as quite perfect for now.

It's not about you flourishing in the future. You are flourishing today.

8. Loneliness

Is solitude the same as loneliness?

'Our language has wisely sensed the two sides of being alone,' writes Paul Tillich. 'It has created the word loneliness to express the pain of being alone. And it has created the word solitude to express the glory of being alone.'

*

I'm glad we're talking about this. Everyone is forever linking solitude with loneliness.

So you heard Lady Gaga?

Yes, she conflated the two. How did she put it?

'I am an artist,' she said. 'We wallow in loneliness and solitude our whole lives... Yes, I'm lonely. But I'm married to my loneliness.'

But you don't equate the two?

No, I think Lady Gaga is mistaken.

It's an easy mistake to make.

Solitude and loneliness can look alike from the outside as both are solitary activities - but there the resemblance ends.

So what's the difference?

Loneliness is a negative state, marked by a sense of isolation.

OK.

When a person is lonely, they feel that something is missing. It's not just about being physically alone; it's possible to be with people and still feel lonely — perhaps the most bitter form of loneliness.

Oh yes.

There is nothing redemptive about this experience. It feels harsh, like a punishment; it's perceived as a state of deficiency provoking discontent and a sense of estrangement in the world.

And solitude?

Solitude is the state of being alone without being lonely; of being happily alone. It's a positive and constructive state of engagement with oneself, and through oneself, with God and the world around. Solitude is something desirable, something to be sought; a state of being alone in the good company of your self.

Everyone's lonely sometimes.

I think that's true. I was first conscious of being lonely on a Christmas day when I was a teenager. No one was around when I wanted them to be. Nothing was happening to fill my day. There was just a silence and I began to feel sorry for myself.

That's stirring echoes in me.

So when did you first feel lonely? And when did you first name it as such?

*

But not all loneliness is about being physically alone?

No, I was struck by the words of a biker called Simon who journeyed through South America. He said this:

'There are times when I have been desperately lonely. It was as if I lived in a bell jar, looking out through the vacuum and glass at the world beyond. Despite being surrounded by friends and family, with company and friendships only a phone call away, you would think it impossible to be lonely living in the town where you where born with opportunities for adventures on most weekends. But in the hours sat at home the loneliness surrounds you. A feeling of emptiness and vacancy; unhappiness in your own company. It is a restlessness that seems impossible to address and facilitates bad decision making.'

That's true.

'But solitude is very different,' he continues. 'Solitude empowers, allows your mind to quiet. The chatter stops, the worries go away and you become happy in your own company.'

So he's known both?

Simon was able to cross the bridge from loneliness to solitude and he did it when he went on a solo bike ride down through South America.

I'm glad for him. But the thing that struck me was this: he was lonely even though he was with people.

Loneliness is not simply a matter of being alone, but the feeling that no one really cares what happens to you. It's the painful awareness that we lack close and meaningful contact with others, which produces feelings of being cut off from them.

The trouble is, many people have been taught loneliness. We want our children to live active lives in the world, and so train them for activity. But if this is the only world they are taught to value, a world of external stimulation, they become alienated from themselves and victims of seeping loneliness and feelings of estrangement.

You mean, we train our children to be lonely through constant entertainment?

It's a diminished education. Does that ring any bells?

*

Everyone feels lonely sometimes but some people feel lonely all the time. Is there anything to be done?

If this is your experience, some quiet and accepting reflection is a good idea. If you are lonely, examine your fears and your attitudes. Get them out in the open.

What sort of things are we talking about?

Have you built walls of defence instead of bridges, for instance? This is common enough. Or are you afraid of closeness with others, afraid of getting hurt or perhaps failing? That's another reason why we hide from people. Or perhaps, because of past experiences, you fear the pain of losing someone you love? Did you once love someone and see them leave?

Those are hard questions.

As Rumi said, 'Your task is not to seek love, but merely to seek and find all the barriers within yourself that you have built against it.'

So loneliness is not something that's done to us; it could be something that unknowingly, we do to ourselves.

We are our psychology, as I said before.

So for the lonely to look at themselves rather than others is not as mad as it sounds?

You could also consider how you spend your time. Are you filling your life by being busy - seeking out and spending time with people you may not particularly like just to stay active and feel involved? That's a recipe for loneliness.

True.

Or do you stuff the spaces in your life with mental noise from the radio, TV, mobile, magazine or internet leaving no room for anything beautiful and self-sustaining to grow inside you? Mental noise makes us dull. No wonder we find ourselves hard to endure.

*

Aldous Huxley had a bleak view of the human experience.

Oh, I know. He believed we're all condemned to perpetual loneliness.

'In spite of language,' he said, 'in spite of intelligence and intuition and sympathy, one can never really communicate anything to anybody.'

That's a pretty bleak view.

He goes on.

I'm not sure I can take it.

He says: 'The essential substance of every thought and feeling remains incommunicable, locked up in the impenetrable strong-room of the individual soul and body. Our life is a sentence of perpetual solitary confinement.'

Powerful words which as I listen sound uncomfortably true.

Maybe. But while acknowledging their force, I don't believe they're the end of the story. Loneliness is not a fixed state but a call to relate to ourselves and the world in a fresh way.

To be fair, that is what Simon the biker found.

Loneliness and solitude are different lands but their borders touch. We walk from one to the other when we cease using others and start allowing ourselves.

Are you able to cross the border now?

9. Information overload

Can information make us ignorant?

Some words from the poet William Wordsworth to set us on the path of solitude today.

Was he the daffodils man?

He was, yes. But here he commends solitude to us:

'When from our better selves we have for too long
Been parted in the hurrying world, and droop,
Sick of its business, of its pleasures tired
How gracious, how benign, is solitude.'

So the question is: what is currently making you droop?

*

One cause of weariness is too much information

I'm sorry, but how can there ever be too much information?

We live in a world of instant information. We can know all sorts of things with just the click of a switch. 'I'll google it,' we say, knowing we're just seconds away from information.

Yep, it's brilliant. I've been researching houses on the internet.

41

So much information! I worked with a girl who knew the height of every model and every actress. 'It's all there on the internet!' she would say to me encouragingly.

Not all information is of equal quality, I suppose.

And sadly, the all-dancing all-singing information highway struggles to give satisfaction for more than five minutes. We spend hours flicking around the internet, discovering this, that and the other, excitedly immersed in what Wordsworth called 'the hurrying world'. Yet at the end of it all, while we know everything, we feel nothing and so we 'droop'.

Was this what you meant at the beginning of our conversation? You said that solitude reconnects us to our inner knowing that isn't the same as our outer knowing.

It's exactly what I meant. It's all about the quality of our knowing and listening with our heart.

❋

I've got to say: humans are very clever and the information highway is remarkable technology.

All true. The trouble is, the information highway tends to feed only the mind and our mind does not need feeding - it needs stilling:

'The mind is restless, turbulent, strong and unyielding,' says the Bhagavad-Gita. 'I consider it as difficult to subdue as the wind.'

So while the internet screen has many uses – like house hunting - leading us into silence is not generally one of them.

❋

I go for a run every morning.

I won't be joining you.

You're not invited; I enjoy the solitude too much. Sometimes I go for long runs. I like my heart pumping, doing what it's there for. I enjoy getting home with exercise in my muscles and if it's been an extra long run then I enjoy feeling shattered. But do you know what I like best of all?

Tell me.

I like the physicality of it, the body-ness of it all. I like the run taking me and shaking me out of my head and into my body.

Why so?

It's never good to be in the head with its mad thoughts; and always good to anchor ourselves in our bodies, the true place of discernment.

Really?

Like with a trained singing voice, true wisdom comes from deep within our body and not from our flibberty-jibberty head.

✲

So a quiet mind is reckoned a precious thing?

'If we have not quiet in our minds,' says John Bunyan, 'outward comfort will do no more for us than a golden slipper on a gouty foot.'

A memorable image.

It's a call to a still mind rather than a racing mind or a condemning mind or a planning mind or an anxious mind or a spinning mind.

And how do we answer that call?

In silence.

In silence?

It's here that we step off the information highway which offers a thousand journeys to nowhere. In silence, we choose not to cooperate with our mental processes and dare to believe there is something beyond them.

How?

Perhaps we use a mantra as a shield to protect us from our thoughts and as a sword to pierce through thoughts.

What sort of mantra? That sounds a bit weird.

A mantra is just a word we choose around which we can gather our inner resources. It should be as short as possible, one word preferably, one syllable preferably, brutally simple like 'Strength' 'Love' 'God' or another of your choice.

Mantras can help?

They're important for some people, less so for others. I've used them when far from physical solitude yet needing to quieten a paranoid mind. A mantra declares our intent to be people beyond thoughts, beyond the oppression of the mental moment wherever we may be.

So a mantra isn't a mental activity.

On the contrary, it expresses the will of our whole body and under-mines the dominance of our bawling-baby mind.

Our bawling-baby mind?

That's what it's like. Using a mantra is like putting a restless baby to sleep, speaking a calming word which settles the bawling child.

So we step off the speeding information highway and discover a slower but perhaps more revealing path?

The path of solitude, yes and you're on the path already.

10. Unborn

How do you receive flattery or criticism?

'I can honestly say – I don't have an ego!' That's what my friend says. Can it be true?

There's a simple test to discover whether your ego is alive and well.

And what's that?

How do you respond to flattery and criticism? If neither has power to affect your friend's mood, then their ego is a small player in their life.

But if we are stirred by flattery or downcast by criticism?

Then our ego remains a significant player in our lives. Egotism requires external prestige to prop up its sense of self and so reacts forcefully to flattery and criticism. Flattery will give it delight for five minutes. Criticism may leave it hobbling for days, years even.

Does any criticism or flattery linger with you?

*

Well, by that reckoning, my friend does have an ego. He won't admit it but criticism puts him in a deep if silent sulk. But then you're born with your ego.

My sense is that you were not born with your ego and that it wasn't always like this. It's another example of us becoming lesser people as we grow up.

How so?

Once we were unborn and quite content. As the unborn, we did not need the validation of others, but were happy simply to be. Maybe you can still sense the echoes of that state in you now; as with distant church bells across a valley, it can still be heard when conditions are right.

*

So solitude is no place for the ego?

On the contrary, we bring all of who we are into our solitude. Nothing is left outside or considered unworthy. And it's here that we recover a right relationship between our ego and our unborn nature.

And what relationship is that?

They need each other but the ego should serve rather than lead. And the trouble is, there's been a role reversal somewhere along the way.

The ego's now in charge?

In a way our ego has kidnapped our unborn-ness and taught it new ways. We need to be aware of this.

What has our ego been teaching us?

Mainly it has taught it this: that true validation only exists in the opinions of others.

I see.

Our unborn selves were wonderfully content and happy just to say 'Here I am!' But then came the shocking reply from the adults around us: 'That is not enough; *you* are not enough.'

From this time on, the ego tried to protect the unborn by guiding us towards the praise and validation of others. After a while, we came to regard this as essential.

There's no harm in a bit of praise.

Praise is wonderful as a gift but dangerous as a requirement. In solitude we move away from this obsession with human validation and cherish instead the purity, freedom and contentment of our unborn nature. To do this, we may abandon our traditional senses in search of fresh and profounder perceptions. As the Taoist poem puts it:

'Close you eyes and you will see clearly
Cease to listen and you will hear the truth.'

*

On reflection, I'm not sure I understand that.

In solitude, we revisit our unborn state; the state we enjoyed before developing our unhealthy obsession with the opinion of others.

Thomas Merton followed a similar path. He sought solitude in order to die to the created things of the world, for it was these things that reminded him of his distance from God. When we were unborn, there were no such barriers and in solitude we hear echoes of this former state and recreate it.

That all sounds a bit frightening. It's like a state of nothingness.

Such talk can create fear. I have seen eyes full of fright when the nothingness of the unborn state is spoken of and this is understandable.

Quite so.

Some fear the lack of boundaries and see their self-image threatened. They may not always like themselves, but at least they know who they are and have a clear image of themselves in their mind.

Which can be reassuring.

On a level, yes. But we note what the ego does: it gives us a self-image and makes us fear life without one. 'If you return to your unborn state, who are you then?' it says. 'What self-image could survive such a return?'

The ego has a point.

Only if you focus on the fear, but we won't do that for as Hafiz says, 'Fear is the cheapest room in the house and I would like to see you living in better conditions.'

So we leave the cheap room?

We've created our self-image out of anxiety and fear. It helped us survive in the past but there comes a time for every child to let go of their security blanket and our self-image is certainly one of those.

Our self-image as a security blanket?

That's about the sum of it.

And beyond our self-image is our unborn state?

'When we were contained within the eternal essence of God,' says Meister Eckhart, 'there was nothing other than God in us. Therefore I say that we should be free of self-knowledge as we were before we were created; that we should allow God to do what he will and that we should be entirely free of all things.'

Your ego may panic a little at such words.

Just a little, yes.

But you could still seek something of the unborn in you today. Try it as you walk towards the bus stop or curl up on the floor and see how it feels.

11. Identity

Will solitude tell me who I am?

Who am I? It seems an important question but can solitude help us with an answer?

I was hoping you'd tell me.

*

I remember the question a listener asked after a talk I'd given.

What was that?

They had a query about their identity. To give a bit of context, I'd been speaking about dismantling the structures of our personality and taking our thoughts less seriously. I'd been saying that truth is less often a shining light from beyond and more often the consciousness of error within; and that spirituality is less about planting large flowers and more about clearing the soil.

That's enough context, I think. I'm beginning to feel like I was there.

And so the question: 'You've said much about what we're not and I understand that, Simon. But if we're not all these things – if we're not our personality and not our thoughts – then what are we? Who are we?'

Good question.

It is and when you ask that question, you are on the way. It's a sign that you're stepping out of the machine and becoming human.

So who am I?

*

Isak Dinesen tells a story from her time in Africa. One day when she was out in the bush, she saw a snake of great beauty with a glistening skin full of wonderful colours. She was so in awe of what she'd seen that she spoke of little else on her return home.

Fair enough.

In an attempt to please her, the house servant then went out into the bush and killed the snake, skinned it and made it into a belt for Isak. But for Isak, there was no beauty there now. The vibrant skin had become dull and grey, because its beauty had not lain in its skin but in its life, its livingness. It was this life that had transformed and permeated the skin.

Fine, but what's that story got to do with anything?

For me, it's a story about identity. Our identity is not what we do or the name we have – but the life beneath.

I see.

I remember when I worked in a supermarket I lost my name badge and had to wear another for six months while waiting for a new one.

So what was your new name?

The name on my new badge was 'Omar' and I was surprised how easily I gave up 'Simon', which I'd been called for half a century, and became 'Omar'.

A name is just another surface label?

Rather than being defined by what we do or our name, our identity is the livingness beneath our skins, the life beneath our labels.

Is this something you can sense now?

*

I suppose the 'Who am I?' question has a long history.

Yes, the issue of identity has exercised philosophers for many centuries.

The 'Bundle' theory comes to mind.

The Bundle theory? Is that what I use when I go to the laundry?

No, it's nothing to do with the weekly wash. It's a theory of self that was spoken of by Hume but anticipated in Buddhism. It offers the idea that there is no single unified self, but rather a variety of experiences and states.

So we're not permanently anything?

You've got it. According to the bundle theory, the enduring self is a fiction, a figment of the ego's imagination. We each have a bundle of experiences but no rope to wrap round them; no binding to bring them to order or hold them together.

That's a pretty unsettling idea.

It can seem so. We're left only with our experiences and no guiding intelligence to make sense of them.

You're not reassuring me.

Others see it differently, however.

You mean they like it?

Well, they think it's truthful and therefore hopeful, because all hope starts with the truth.

So how is it hopeful?

They sense in these ideas a present adventure for every human. Each of us becomes a constant act of creation, with every moment drawing and asking new things from us. The king or queen in us dies daily; and the new king or queen is enthroned daily.

That does make some sense.

So in this moment, you're a rich gathering of your unique experiences, kindly given some shape by your ego.

'Kindly'?

I say kindly, because we all need shape to proceed in the world, we all need a rope around our bundle – even if it's imaginary.

But we don't worship the rope.

We never imagine we're defined for life by its knots. And in solitude, we sometimes undo the rope because it cannot hold our livingness for long without beginning to kill.

*

The questioner after my talk was right.

You don't tend to speak about who we are?

No, I prefer to reflect on who we are not.

Why so?

If I ask 'Who am I?' I start to create something phoney, some gratifying fiction. But if I remember who I am not, then what I am emerges naturally and without falsification.

We just have to remember not to give this creation a name.

That would be like pinning a butterfly to the wall and calling it flight. But I'll leave you to your solitude now. You needn't take your self image with you.

12. Nature

What do you do with nature?

I live above a pub on a noisy London street that quietens only around 3.00am for a couple of hours. When not at home, I spend much of my time pressed inside a busy London tube. On my return home, large piles of uncollected rubbish sit in the down-at-heel alley way that leads to my disintegrating stone staircase.

So it's not the Lake District.

It isn't. Yet daily I delight in nature, which is a constant revelation of strength, beauty, endurance, fragility, new birth and change. One of the reasons the staircase is disintegrating is that apparently fragile flowers force their way through the concrete. Life will not be thwarted.

Nature is good for us?

And a gift. Aware of the pressures life places on us we help ourselves by becoming contemplatives of our own back yard, wherever it happens to be.

*

I remember a woman on a packed tube train.

What was memorable about her?

Her luggage. Amid the strained and anxious faces in the carriage at the end of a working day, she had a huge yellow flower on her lap.

Hah!

In the circumstances the plant seemed almost god-like. Its colourful carefree simplicity and delight were entirely at odds with the prevailing mood and invited us all into a different way of being.

How do you mean?

As I contemplated the flower, I found myself smiling.

It was drawn out of you.

Without my knowing, yes – there I was, smiling on the tube. And I hope as the journey progressed, the flower's qualities became mine, became me.

Contemplating the flower led you into a moment of solitude on the busy tube?

Once we set our compass towards silence, creation conspires to help us.

✻

We're reflecting on nature.

We are.

And in Karen Armstrong's book, *Buddha*, she includes the story of a depressed king who is travelling through a park full of huge trees. He gets out and starts to examine their massive roots.

To what end?

He discovers they inspire trust and confidence in him:

'They were quiet,' says the Buddhist scriptures, 'no discordant voices disturbed their peace; they gave out a sense of being apart from the ordinary world, a place where one could take refuge from people and find a retreat from the cruelties of life. Looking at these wonderful old trees, the King was reminded immediately of the Buddha and drove for miles to the house where the Buddha was staying.'

What's in that story for you?

Spirituality is the art of making connections and I enjoy that process taking place here. In solitude, a king finds great strength and peace in the tree roots. The roots draw him into a profounder experience of trust. He then remembers that he has also found such qualities in a person and goes to seek him out.

*

I suppose in a noisy world nature is at least nice and peaceful.

Really? When did you last go for a walk?

I confess I'm not really one for the great outdoors.

People talk about the silence of nature, but in truth, it's often a pretty noisy affair. From water falls to thunder, bird song to wind in the trees nature is not always quiet - but can bring us to inner quiet.

How?

It's just so life-stoppingly present; that's my feeling.

'Seek to be alone much to commune with nature,' writes Walter Russell, 'and be thus inspired by her mighty whisperings within your consciousness.'

I'm not sure about the 'mighty whisperings'.

You should definitely get out more, and sometimes, go alone. As Russell continues, 'Nature is a most jealous god, for she will not whisper her inspiring revelations to you unless you are absolutely alone with her.'

So nature doesn't want to share me?

That's right. Sometimes she asks for our solitary and undivided attention.

And so demands that we leave people behind.

And this isn't always easy. A friend of mine was once a member of a house party in Wales. One evening, he knew he needed to be alone. He got up out of his chair and said, 'I'm going out for a while – I need to be alone.'

The young man sitting next to him also stood up. 'Yes, I need to be alone as well,' he said. 'Can I come with you?'

✳

Is there anything wrong with going for a walk with someone in the countryside?

Not at all. It can be a delight. But we notice that it's different; it's not solitude.

How do you mean?

Perhaps they say something like 'Isn't that flower wonderful?' or 'Just look at that cloud!'

So?

It's a borrowed experience. The flower or the cloud – it's their experience, not ours. They're directing our attention to their experiences, and direction from others is something we leave behind in solitude.

I see.

In solitude, we have our own experiences as creation conspires to speak with us and help us. We will not borrow experiences of nature from others, however well-meaning. We will be those who experience it for our selves.

✳

A number of chapters of this book were scribbled in rough on holiday beneath a large mountain. The mountain was a constant presence, neither validating me nor criticising me. It was just there, immoveable, dry and quite timeless. It looks no different now to how it would have looked thousands of years ago.

And did it help?

I suspect it did. The mountain didn't invite relationship for as we were told by the locals, it was inhabited by scorpions and snakes. Yet it was a constant companion, both amid the bright sun and the star-spangled nights. I appreciate and aspire to its constancy.

*

We'll not get sentimental about nature, though.

No, that's always a mistake.

Speak to a farmer or flood victim and they'll tell you of its savagery and unpredictiability.

Nature is not all fluffy clouds, daisy chains and fields of lilac.

But in solitude, it draws us out of ourselves and then kindly returns us in some way reborn. Wherever we live, we can understand Lord Byron:

There is pleasure in the pathless wood,
There is a rapture on the lonely shore
There is a society where none intrudes
By the sea and music is its roar.
I love not man the less but nature more.

13. Silence

How do you relate to silence?

Solitude is the walk into inner silence.

So silence is golden?

Not necessarily.

Why not?

For the simple reason that not all silence is the same; indeed much of it is low-grade in quality.

How do you mean?

Think of the different silences. There's the surly silence of sulk and rage, shocked silence, angry silence, anxious silence, judging silence, scheming silence, mind-spinning silence.

Yes, I can see the variety of low-grade possibilities.

And if we're honest, sometimes one of these is all we can manage when we first embark on the adventure of solitude.

So what does your silence feel like now?

*

In a way, the answer doesn't matter.

I'm still thinking about it.

Good. Listen to your body as well, by the way; that's revealing about the nature of your silence.

OK.

What's important is that you notice the present nature of your inscape. What's bothering you?

There is something, actually.

Well, a moment or two of quiet reflection on the nature of your silence and perhaps you can trace back from your feelings and find the cause.

And the point of this?

Once we know these things – once we've acknowledged that we are angry or fearful about something and have acknowledged what it is – then we can begin to move beyond this troubled silence into the deeper and more profound silence of listening.

But first, we may have to remove some obstacles?

That's right. As I often say, you have to say hello to something before you can say goodbye to it.

Yes, you do often say that.

*

Here's a vision of silence from Rabindrath Tagore:

'Let my doing nothing, when I have nothing to do, become untroubled in its depth of peace like the evening in the seashore when the water is silent.'

That is a beautiful vision.

It is. Tagore describes something still, deep and peaceful so we will breathe that in.

But beware of something.

What should I beware of?

Be careful you don't allow its beauty to become a stick with which to beat yourself.

How do you mean?

The silence Tagore speaks of is generally the result of a search and the transcending of obstacles. It's the end of a journey rather than something conjured up by clever technique. No other soul can give us such a silence as this and we cannot always find it ourselves.

But at least we glimpse our destination.

That's right. We understand the image of still waters in the evening; flecked with light, still and deep. And sometimes we've known that in ourselves.

That's true, surprisingly.

And so we push back the foliage with our hand and carry on down the path.

*

How can we help ourselves in this?

Outer silence can be an aid to cultivating inner silence.

I was once, to my surprise, caught up in a wonderful cathedral silence.

Yes, we can be surprised by silence.

And suddenly I'm noticing a lot of surprise on this page.

And your problem?

No problem. It's quite invigorating!

Surprise and solitude are very close.

*

But returning to your question, not everyone wishes to put themselves in a quiet place.

Why is that?

Some people find silence threatening. They must have music playing as they walk or the radio talking at all times. Some must have the TV on in their room as they go to sleep.

Which is not really a recipe for inner quiet.

No. For these people, the quest for inner silence will start a little further back with the question: why is outer silence so frightening? Why does it make me uncomfortable?

Presumably it's something in their past.

True. Here in their adult life is a damaged echo from way back and to understand that echo is helpful. When we were small, we may have had good reason to find silences difficult. Perhaps there are scenes we remember in silence or anxious feelings that come to the surface.

And if they do?

We'll be kind to these feelings and hear them out. The child within has carried them all these years and has wished to speak of them for so long.

And so we listen to the child?

We do. We're always listening for the child, because when the child's heard, we're able to move on a little. Perhaps for five or ten minutes a day we begin to walk free; we dare a little outer silence and hear there something of the inner silence we've been denied. It's a sort of homecoming.

*

So outer silence helps?

Undoubtedly. As we begin to allow outer silence, inner silence comes to greet us, even if it's tentative at first. Perhaps we could ally our minds with a peaceful scene as Tagore did. He described a silent seashore. I sometimes remember a huge fjord in Norway – spacious, still and deep. In solitude, as in life, these are characteristics I aspire to.

*

You talked about low-quality silence.

There's a lot of it about.

So what is high quality silence?'

High quality silence is still, empty, listening, hopeful; wordless hope.

But we're using words.

Words can help on the path of solitude, so we might use words along the way. Perhaps they get us onto the path in the first place, just as music might. But at some point we will leave them behind, their job done. In many ways, words interrupt the language of creation and can hold us back from hearing.

'Listen in deep silence,' advises *A Course in Miracles*. 'Be very still and open your mind. Sink deep into the peace that waits for you beyond the frantic, riotous thoughts and sights and sounds of this insane world.'

*

62

Is inner silence just a private pleasure?

Far from it. And as we begin to experience inner silence, we are soon offering it back to the world.

How does that work?

Various experiments around the world have revealed that if you put even a relatively small number of people who meditate into a troubled area, it significantly lowers the aggression-fuelled violence there.

Peace spills out?

Yes, it's a mystery but it's also a fact. The presence of peace changes the social climate.

So perhaps my solitude can be good for the world?

Undoubtedly. Our solitude changes the world around us. Back in the crowd, we find ourselves speaking from the sanity of silence rather than from the jangling noise of our restless agendas.

We take our solitude and silence into the world.

But first the silence. You could walk towards it now.

14. Spontaneity

Can we become spontaneous people?

I have a question.

I'm ready.

Well, I have a quotation first and then a question.

I'm still ready.

'There is no limit to what a man can do or where he can go if he doesn't mind who gets the credit,' said Robert W. Woodruff, one-time CEO at Coca-Cola.

Interesting. And the question?

Is your life a determined seeking after credit?

*

There aren't many people on earth who don't want some credit for what they do.

True. In school, we're taught to take credit for the work we do – and shame for our failures - and we take this attitude into life.

Having said that, some are definitely more grasping for credit than others.

Yes, they possess this need in an extreme form. They desire all the credit and therefore struggle to give any to anyone else. If there's credit being handed out, they want everything - like someone grabbing a treasure trove and saying 'It's all mine!'

And then there are others who are not so demanding.

These are the ones who are happy enough in a team and open to applauding others. They can say 'Well done!' without feeling sick inside. But they also want credit where it's due.

Oh, yes.

If the boss starts claiming it was his idea when it wasn't his idea, then even the team player can be angry. 'Credit where it's due' is a maxim most of us live by, which includes credit being paid into our account occasionally.

So what is this need for credit all about?

Behind this need is a sense of deficiency. In those desperate for credit, there is a gaping hole of need. In those seeking an average amount of credit, it's a manageable sense of deficiency but present nonetheless.

Is anyone hurt by this?

One of the saddest losses for credit-hunters is the gift of spontaneity. Constantly aware of what's due to them, their inner life becomes a very narrow band of possibility.

How do you mean?

I think of the famous violinist who on one occasion was applauded for his rendition of a Beethoven violin concerto. Everyone wanted to know how he did it. 'I have splendid music,' he said, 'a splendid violin and a splendid bow. All I need to do is bring them together and get out the way.'

Not your average celebrity response.

I like the idea of us getting out of the way of what we do. And it's perhaps the best definition of spontaneity.

How so?

We do what we do to earn a living; we do what we do to look after those around us; we even do what we do in pursuit of a long term goal. But we do all these things with a sense of inner space, because the space has been vacated by ourselves.

There's a vacant space once occupied by our ego?

That's the hope. And where this space exists, we can be spontaneous, free to change direction, to go with something new, because there are no strings attached to our actions.

I do not need credit; I am not there.

*

One of the healing joys of solitude is that we're free there from the world's definitions of us.

How do you mean?

People stick all sorts of labels and assessments on us as we go about our business. But when we close the door on the world in solitude, these labels and assessments – though they may bang angrily on the door at first - are shut out.

They have no place there?

Exactly. And perhaps in time, as we experience solitude more deeply, we will become free not only of the world's definitions of ourselves but also of our own definitions of ourselves, which are much more damaging.

Such as?

Such as noting the gnawing sense of deficiency which so demands the affirmation of others, demands credit where it's due - and even credit where it's not due.

But be honest - why would anyone want to notice deficiency in them selves?

For one very good reason: a sense of deficiency is a scream from our past. It needs listening to if we wish to be free.

*

We started this chapter with a quotation.

I wrote it down: 'There is no limit to what a man can do or where he can go if he doesn't mind who takes the credit.'

Whether this is true in business, I'm not sure; but it's true in life for it describes a free soul, a spontaneous soul which has been vacated by the ego.

The angels dance on such a stage.

15. Love and Hate

What barriers to love have I erected?

In the growing of love, there is no better garden than the garden of solitude. It's best nurtured, however, not by flowery thoughts but in the removal of hatred from our lives.

That's not very romantic!

*

'Hell is other people,' said Jean-Paul Sartre.

True.

Partially true.

Why so?

Other people are hell only when we are hell to ourselves. When we accept ourselves then others can't bring hell to our door.

You mean how I regard others depends on how I regard myself?

Undoubtedly. But we understand Sartre's words; it's hard not to hate people, though some find it hard to admit.

How do you mean?

Some will deny what they feel because they think it's sinful. Perhaps strong angry feelings were not allowed inside them as children and so they continue to deny them now. 'You ought not to hate people, so I don't,' they say.

I think a lot of people deny their true feelings for just that reason.

It's called 'a hardening of the oughteries' and it has consequences. Perhaps they bury their hate deep down inside where in time it becomes depression.

You think so?

Others rationalise their dark feelings and give them another name – a name which makes them appear honourable. They say something like: 'I have no particular feelings about Jim one way or another - I just find his behaviour very disappointing.'

Oh, I recognise that! A friend of mine will say she was saddened by something, disappointed by something, bemused – anything instead of using the word 'angry'! She can never use that word.

Emotionally, she is still the little girl who received the message that anger is wrong; that she ought not to be angry. She will struggle to admit to it now.

So what do we do?

Probably the best approach to hatred is to acknowledge it honestly. We acknowledge that we hate our parents, son, boss, colleague, golf partner or whoever – and then give up.

Give up?

This may sound defeatist and it is. But if we want to love more and hate less then it's best that we give up the fight, put down our sword, rest our aching arm and admit we can fight no more. Reluctantly, we accept that the hatred will stay with us until we die, so what is the point in continuing the struggle?

69

I can't believe I'm hearing this.

It's strange but help often comes when we admit defeat, when we finally raise the white flag.

Explain.

It's when we can deny our feelings no longer and can fight our feelings no longer that assistance arrives. It comes like a knight on horseback to scoop the frightened child to safety from the barking dogs and snarling bears of our unmanageable feelings.

You could try giving up now.

*

Can we get on to love now?

I'm talking about hate when I'm supposed to be reflecting on love, but there's a reason for this. Love is best nurtured not by the flowery construction of sweet thoughts but the steady dismantlement of hatred in our lives.

You've said that.

And it's still true. The quality of love in a person is not measured by their relationship with their husband, wife, partner, children or dad; it's measured by the absence of hatred for the world.

I'm not sure many will agree with you there.

It's the stranger's love. As the anonymous writer of *The Cloud of Unknowing* says, 'The perfect worker has no special regard for any particular person whether relative or stranger, friend or foe. He thinks of them all alike as his kinsmen and none as strangers. He sees all as friends and none as enemies.'

That's certainly different. Most love I see is pretty tribal and possessive.

Whereas with this love there is no pay-off. There's no 'You scratch my back I'll scratch yours.' This love exists freely and without boundaries in the world and is given free of charge, whether it's to the man reading our electricity metre, our mother or the local Imam.

As Herman Hesse said: 'The only thing of importance to me is being able to love the world without looking down on it, without hating it and myself – being able to regard it and myself and all beings with love, admiration and reverence.'

Now that's ambition for you.

*

What about special friends?

We'll all have special friendships. Buddha had Ananda and Jesus had Mary Magdalene. But if our love becomes squeezed into those at the expense of others, if it becomes preferential or possessive, then it becomes a small and sickly thing. We cherish everyone but possess no one.

So where's solitude in all this?

In solitude we nurture love by noticing our hostility. Hostility will arise in us as we allow silence in ourselves; petty hatreds will be eager to fill the space.

This is normal?

This is quite normal and our response is always the same: we greet each hatred, each hostile thought, speak with them awhile and then allow them to disperse. As they disperse, love grows in the soil space they leave behind. It's a love that will extend from our solitude into the world beyond.

Seeping love?

That's a nice phrase. As Sir Francis Bacon said, 'Little do men perceive what solitude is and how far it extendeth. For a crowd is not company and faces are but a gallery of pictures and talk but a tinkling cymbal, where there is no love.'

16. After Eden

Why do people feel alone?

In the third chapter of Genesis, right at the beginning of the Hebrew Scriptures, we find the story of Adam and Eve in the Garden of Eden.

Why are you telling me this?

Because I think it's an important story.

I've never thought of it as particularly important. And obviously it's a myth. So why does it interest you?

The story describes a change in Adam and Eve's circumstances and it happens after they eat an apple from the Tree of Knowledge.

So what changes?

Everything! Before this event, Adam and Eve are a couple at one with each other and with their God. After the event, they become a couple conscious only of their difference and hiding from God.

How do we know that?

It's there in the story. Previously, their happy nakedness spoke of their unity with each other in a relationship where nothing was hidden. But afterwards, they become ashamed of their difference and cover their genitals which must now become secret. They hide from each other.

And God?

It's the same with him. Previously they had enjoyed direct communion with God in the garden. But afterwards, they hide from God so
he can't find them. 'Where are you?' asks God, who's a bit surprised at
their absence as they've never gone missing before.

*

But as I say, it's a myth!

It may be a myth; but it's a myth with much to say about the human
race.

*So the story of Adam and Eve in the Garden of Eden tells us a primal
truth?*

It's telling us that the human race has become separate from itself and
the natural order. The story describes the origins of loneliness and the
reasons why we fear it.

Even though it's not historically true?

People have strong opinions about that, but it's not important. What
matters more than the historical truth is the emotional truth.

This story is emtionally true?

Yes. Somehwere in our distant memory, we, like Adam and Eve, feel
evicted from the Garden of Eden, evicted from oneness with our world
and cut adrift.

*

*I can feel some truth in that. But if we want to get back together with
everyone, how on earth is solitude going to help?*

Do you have time?

I have time, yes.

73

The human is an unusual mammal.

In what way?

Consider this amazing creature. He is life being aware of itself.

True.

But the miracle of this awareness brings pain as well as delight. Here is a creature aware of itself and others, aware of past and future time, aware of relationships, possibilities, longings and regret; and painfully aware of death, that time is running out.

That is quite a burden.

I agree. So it's small wonder that we have mental health issues. Like Adam in the garden, we panic at such awareness, cover up and hide. Some hide in dependence, becoming clingy; others opt for isolation. But whichever direction we run in, all paths lead to separation – separation from others and separation from ourselves.

So our panic leaves us unconscious; surrounded by people maybe, but separate from them and therefore unconscious?

*

How can solitude help?

Have you still got time?

Yes, I have time.

And energy?

Maybe.

Then consider: when we think of our lives, we think of the content.

How do you mean?

This is the stuff we might talk about at the end of the day or chat over on the phone. We perceive our life as our situation, our relationships, our job, our prospects, plans or interests.

Of course. What else could our life be?

These things are not our life.

Come again?

They are merely the hooks upon which we hang our life. Our life is our consciousness.

Our consciousness?

Yes, the consciousness you spoke of just now. Our life is not what happens to us but how we perceive what happens to us - or our consciousness.

OK, I think I'm with you.

So for someone or something to enter my life, I have to be conscious of them. It's this consciousness, this awareness which touches me and is my true life. 'Life is only real when I am,' as Gurdjieff says.

And the story of the Garden of Eden is about this consciousness - this awareness of others - being damaged?

Exactly. I am not with someone when I sit next to them; I am with them when I am conscious of them. When we cease to be conscious of people, we hide from them in some way, separate from them in some way.

So just being with people isn't the answer to our loneliness?

On one level, other people's actions and qualities can touch me, some-times delightfully. But in another way, they do not. It's my experience of their actions which touches me, my consciousness of them; and here is the healing and connecting power of solitude.

In solitude, we become more conscious of life and therefore more able both to receive and give?

I believe so. In solitude we become reacquainted with our conscious selves, enabling us to connect with people rather than separate from them. If we are conscious, there is no need to hide.

*

We close with a poem by Hafiz which speaks of both separation and union and has the scent of Eden in its lines:

'When the words stop and you can't endure the silence,
That reveals your heart's pain,
Or emptiness,
Or that great wrenching-sweet longing.

That is the time to try and listen to what the beloved's eyes
Most want
To
Say.'

17. Listening

Have you ever listened for someone?

I'm sitting on some stones on the Greek island of Rhodes.

That's nice for you.

I've turned down the donkey ride and walked up many steps to reach the Acropolis in Lindos.

Old stones?

These particular stones are over 2000 years old. On each one, precise lettering is carved in ancient script; and I'm wondering if I can meet the craftsman who did it.

How are you going to do that?

✳

Let's go back in time. The craftsman with his chisel and hammer in 400 BC probably never imagined his words would be read in 2011 AD; or that his skill would be appreciated so many years and generations down the line.

I suspect not. He probably wasn't thinking much beyond his tea.

And as for an Englishman being here, that would have been quite beyond his understanding. While Rhodians were building this remarkable temple, the English were still in mud huts, a backward people unknown beyond their own front door.

So why are you telling me this?

To begin with, as I sat there, this was the way I was thinking. I felt only a chasm of difference between the craftsman and myself.

Which there is.

But as I began to listen, I could hear his chiselling and could smell his sweat in the heat of the midday sun. Time melted and then it seemed that instead of a chasm of difference, everything linked us together.

Why the change?

This tends to happen when we listen to others, whatever century they lived. We may hear difference to begin with but it tends to become connection.

It may work with history. It doesn't work with those who are still alive.

I think it does.

An example?

I remember Jane in Liverpool. When Jane returned to the office after some solitude and a sandwich in the park, she changed her approach to her boss.

So what had been going on?

It had not been a happy morning. Jane was furious with the way her boss had spoken to her that morning and with good reason.

Don't tell me - after some solitude, she decided to let it all go and say nothing?

Not at all. Jane returned from her lunch time solitude very clear what she must do. She still needed to speak to her boss about the way he had treated her. So when they met at 2.30pm she expressed herself very clearly.

Go, Jane, go!

But the difference was this: by allowing her solitude to become listening she spoke calmly because she was not speaking to an enemy.

So who was she speaking to?

She was speaking to someone with whom she now had connection. She'd found this connection by allowing her solitude to become listening; listening for the person.

There had been no sense of connection between them at 10.00am.

And how did her boss respond?

He couldn't cope with her words. He turned his sense of shame into denial, accepting no responsibility and told her it was a fuss about nothing.

Frustrating for Jane.

Yes. It's hard to listen for people when they're not listening to themselves. Not even God can relate to an unexamined life.

So what did she do?

Jane breathed in deeply and took herself away to recover. In solitude we allow the non-listening of others to pass through us rather than lodge in us.

*

What helps listening?

Silence helps listening - both outer silence and inner silence. As Alice Koller describes it, silence is like a cloak she flings over herself and covers herself with:

'I surround myself with silence,' she writes. 'The silence is within me, permeates my house, reaches beyond the surfaces of the outer walls and into the bordering woods. It is one silence, continuous from within me outward in all directions: above, beneath, forward, rearward, sideward. In the silence I listen, I watch, I sense, I attend, I observe. I require this silence, I search it out.'

A hunter of silence!

And you?

*

As we listen for others in our deepening silence, we may also listen to ourselves with a new honesty.

We don't tend to listen to ourselves very well.

Probably not. We imagine everyone else is the problem so what is there to take note of in ourselves?

Yep, that's me.

But in the safety of the developing silence, as layers of myth-making dissolve, a listening spirit emerges within us that's able to hear the emptiness of our boasts and more particularly, the needy soul behind our claims.

As we dismantle our own self-righteousness it creates a space in which we hear more, assume less and find connections with others?

*

And out of listening comes true obedience.

That's not a word I like.

And maybe with good reason. But the English word *obedience* comes from the Latin word *audire*, which means *to listen*. The spiritual life creates a listening space within us out of which obedience to truth and life can grow.

18. Knowing or understanding?

Can you know everything and understand nothing?

The Russian émigré P.D. Ouspensky once wrote a book called *Tertium Organum*.

I confess, I haven't read it.

You and many others. It translates as *The Third Canon of Thought* and claimed to be 'a key to the enigmas of the world'.

Ambitious.

But after it was published, his mentor G.I. Gurdjieff said this to him: 'If you understand everything you have written in your book, I take my hat off to you.'

I'm glad he liked it.

But did he?

It sounds like a compliment to me.

Well, it does at first, but on reflection – and knowing Gurdjieff a little - I sense it's something else. The implication between the lines is that even though he knew it all, he probably didn't understand it all.

That's a surprising idea. I mean, you'd have thought that the one implies the other; that if you know something you understand it.

Experience suggests otherwise. I remember a boy at school. He knew every football statistic on the planet. Who won the cup when; which team got relegated in 1961; which left back had played the most times for his country etc etc.

I sense a 'but' in the air.

The 'but' is this: he couldn't play the game and had no interest in playing the game. He'd never stepped onto a pitch, never sweated his way through a match, never taken a tackle and had no sense of what made for good football.

He could tell you how many goals a centre forward scored last season; but not the particular skills he brought to the game?

That's right. He was a football insider as regards knowledge, but an outsider in his understanding. He hadn't lived it. And of course a couple of years later he gave up all interest in football and went off to acquire knowledge about something else.

I see. It was the knowledge that made him feel secure in the world; the subject matter was less important.

Indeed.

But is that so bad? Sounds pretty harmless really.

It's about our level of engagement with our surroundings, inner and outer. I was once told someone had 'an encyclopaedic knowledge of the world'.

And did they?

It turned out they knew the capital city and population figures of every country.

Impressive in its way.

On a level, yes. But he knew nothing of the countries themselves – nothing of their history, faith, struggles and hopes.

You speak as if knowledge and understanding hardly have a relationship.

They're separate callings.

Separate callings?!

I remember a psychology student I met. She knew every famous psychologist, every theory of human behaviour and every analytical label under the psychological sun. But do you know what?

What?

I never sensed she understood people or that as we talked she was making any attempt to understand me. She was not a person I'd have revealed anything to for there was no receiving place inside her.

That's ringing some bells.

No doubt she passed her exams with flying colours, however, and is now an expert in human behaviour somewhere!

Do I detect a little bitterness?

I'd call it anger. It's one thing for an awkward boy to opt for knowledge over understanding at school in order to survive; but it's more dangerous in the healing professions which can quickly become a way of keeping my self from my self.

You mean, I become an expert in the theory of healing in order to avoid my own healing?

It happens and it's the best cover of all. I feel good about myself while avoiding myself.

So knowledge actually becomes a means of denial, a means of avoiding our true feelings.

To know something requires only a small part of our intellectual selves; to understand something requires a connection with our whole selves, mind, body and will. I can discover the capital city of a country at no cost to my emotional self. But to understand a country, something in me must die. I must leave the land of my experience and enter into the land of theirs.

So if you're to bring healing to others?

You start with your own heart. The path of solitude asks that you leave behind the labels and psychological theories and risk visiting your own land. 'Physician, heal thyself' as they saying goes.

As opposed to 'Physician, avoid thyself.'

*

This is now bringing to mind a popular speaker I once heard.

He'd been recommended?

Oh, everyone loved him but for some reason I felt uncomfortable as I listened. I couldn't fault anything he said, but it was a bit like Gurdjieff said earlier: I had no sense that they understood it and so it sounded cheap. Yes, that's the word – cheap.

*

We must face facts: knowledge slickly presented sells well today.

And understanding?

You can't sell understanding because that's a personal journey.

The world prefers knowledge.

It prefers knowledge because it's less threatening. On the horizontal and short-term scale of day-to-day life, where information is worshipped, knowledge comes before understanding.

But in the vertical and eternal scale, where the stronger and deeper truth lies, understanding is all that matters.

Because?

Because only in understanding do we connect with the truth of ourselves. One of the reasons why the world of self-help is such a restless and frustrated world is that it races from one exciting theory to another without ever connecting to its crying self.

It uses knowledge to avoid understanding?

It can do, because as I've said, understanding comes at a price. Knowledge is cheap and easily gathered from the surface. But understanding is a treasure found only in the deeper waters.

Another example?

I often say to clients, 'You know it all!' They nod their heads with sadness, aware that they do but that somehow it isn't enough. They often know more than me and can list theories I've never heard of.

But their knowledge isn't helping.

It's about connection. When they put their knowledge down and listen for the child, then I know they're in the foothills of understanding.

It's almost about going back to the beginning.

'Stop thinking and talking about it and there is nothing you will not be able to know,' is the Zen advice.

Like a child learning to walk, falteringly we relearn what it means to live the moment rather than killing it with our knowledge. We learn to trust life rather than theories and discover there a surprising strength, a growing courage and a changing shape to our heart – brief pictures of Eden.

So in your solitude today, try leaving your knowledge outside. Take only the child.

19. Balance

Have you lost your balance?

We live in a fast moving world.

The world spins no faster today than it did in ancient times but perhaps technology makes it feel like it does.

Agreed.

Our e mails and tweets whizz around the planet in seconds; news is with us almost before it happens while a 24-hour media machine and social networking sites swamp us with more information than is either decent or healthy.

You're making me giddy.

Losing your balance, perhaps?

*

In conditions such as these, it can be hard to keep our balance. Drunk on mental stress we stagger from one sort of noise to another sort of noise.

Around us, imbalance is the norm; within us, mind, body and soul fight like soldiers in the dark, blind to the fact they're all on the same side. In such a setting, it's a challenge to stay standing and to walk the straight line of sanity.

All rather dramatic, but I think I take your drift. So how do we know if we've lost our balance?

A clear sign of our loss of balance is the obsessions we develop. In the absence of wholeness, we start to have strong feelings about unimportant things; we develop small-time obsessions to distract us from our uncomfortable state.

Why?

We look to our obsessions to give us meaning.

Like Obsessive Compulsive Disorder?

That's one form of obsession but there are many others and they're unpleasant gods who bring more unhappiness than joy.

*

So which gods do I worship?

That is your investigation. Your obsessions are not mine and mine are not yours, but they're alike in one way: they ruin our lives and make us foolish.

How?

Someone with an obsession is like a man whose right leg is twice as long as his left leg. He walks with a considerable tilt and will proceed with pain and difficulty often falling over.

So why don't we get rid of them?

Obsessions present themselves as something utterly essential. They appear as things that we cannot put down, as part of who we are. And so it is that we return to them 'like a dog returns to its vomit.'

That's a bit harsh.

It is a savage old adage but psychologically accurate. We do return again and again to things that make us ill.

And solitude helps?

'Who looks outside, dreams; who looks inside, awakes.'

Jung?

*

I'm reminded of the story of Compulsi.

Who's he?

Compulsi was the greatest tailor in the world. So when Ewan wanted a new suit he went straight to Compulsi as the best man for the job.

Compulsi was reassuring when they met. He expertly measured Ewan and told him to return in two weeks when his suit would be ready.

Two weeks later Ewan returned and Compulsi produced the suit for him to try on. At first sight, it looked fantastic and Ewan changed into it eagerly.

But strangely, it did not feel quite right. The left shoulder of the jacket was much smaller than the right. The waist coat was too tight causing discomfort, while the trousers were simply too long and dragged along the floor.

'How is my creation?' asked Compulsi.

'It's wonderful!' said Ewan politely. But he did mention the small left shoulder, the tight waist coat and the over-long trousers. Compulsi was not pleased.

'What!?' he cried. 'Are you questioning my craftsmanship?'

'Oh, no, not at all, not at all!' said Ewan, mortified at upsetting the world's greatest tailor. 'Everything is fine! No, really!'

And everything was fine as Ewan left the shop in his new suit and walked down the road. It was fine as long as he stooped awkwardly to his left to accommodate the tight shoulder; held his breath to ease the tightness of the waist coat and skipped and jumped uncomfortably on tip toe to lessen the impact of the over-long trousers.

What a wonderful suit! He wore it again and again. And over time, Ewan became quite used to this new way of walking – even if to the outsider, it all looked slightly strange.

*

And the point is?

We walk through this life in an odd manner because we've accepted our obsessions, like Ewan accepted his ridiculous suit. We begin to imagine they're normal, harmless and with us forever.

Like a dog, we return to our vomit?

We do. But our obsessions are a disease, born out of our unhappiness.

So how do we handle them?

With gentleness. They need healing and to that end, they need our kindness. Listen to your obsession. What is at the root of it? What is it trying to say? What gave birth to this dull demon? He's a silly little fellow but with a mean streak and can cause terrible trouble.

And born out of unhappiness, you say?

Always, always, always.

An example?

Perhaps you're obsessed with judging people. If you are, then a long time ago you too felt judged. When you were small, you were made to feel terrible when judged by a parent. Now you judge others to deflect the blame you felt back then.

Even now?

Yes. You're still trying to make yourself feel better, feel less judged and appear in the world as the one in the right.

If only we could be saved from our perceptions! It's our perceptions which leave us unbalanced.

I think you're right and I find the words of the Dalai Lama helpful in that regard: 'I find hope in the darkest of days and focus in the brightest. I don't judge the universe.'

Our false perceptions arise out of our false judgements. We panic in the dark days and draw mistaken conclusions, just as we get hysterical on the good days and make equally false assessments.

His words bring balance to me when I can live them.

Yes, it's one thing to know them – quite another to own them.

*

I like that Pascal quote in the introduction.

Remind me.

'All men's miseries derive from not being able to sit quiet in a room alone.'

Yes, that is quite startling.

I've heard our unhappiness blamed on many things, but never that!

It's about the courage to endure your superficial self and allow a deepening silence.

And that helps?

Such silence brings balance to mind, body and spirit. The mad gusts of wind settle into a still day within. It's the end of unhappiness.

For a moment, we remove Compulsi's suit?

Definitely. In solitude we recover our poise and find a surer walk. In this place, the tight knots of our obsessions press less painfully into our skin, and we become what they distracted us from: courage, dignity, self-control, spaciousness, strength –

- and balance.

20. Action

Do my actions sow good
seed in the world?

In solitude, we look after our actions.

Why do that?

They need looking after: for through our actions, we impregnate the world.

So we're considering our actions: are they good seed?

*

Who has the most problems with solitude?

It's activists who have most problems with solitude, though it is they who need it the most.

Why?

Our actions impregnate the world for good or ill, so the roots of those actions are worth considering.

An example?

Take Hitler and St Francis of Assisi.

Not two characters often found in the same sentence.

They're remembered for what they did.

They certainly are.

But their actions did not appear by chance. What they did was the outcome of their thoughts, which varied in quality.

You're saying that if our solitude is sick, then so are our actions.

And if our solitude is well, then so are our deeds. As Jesus said, 'The good man brings good things out of the good stored up in his heart and the evil man brings evil things out of the evil stored up in his heart. For out of the overflow of his heart, his mouth speaks.'

Our words and actions are an overflow of our heart. That's a bit scary!

In our solitude, we look after our thoughts and thereby nurse our actions back to health.

And in our lack of solitude?

In our lack of solitude we abandon our words and actions to indifference, carelessness and stupidity.

Ouch!

*

Let's consider two ways in which solitude can give grace, clarity and strength to our actions.

That sounds like a good idea. I'm still recovering from your last observation.

First, we learn to respond rather than react.

There's a difference?

There's a big difference between reactive action and responsive action. I have written elsewhere about these two (*Enneagram: A private session with the world's greatest psychologist*) and so I will be brief on the subject here.

I like brevity. What is it they say to speakers? 'If you haven't struck oil in ten minutes, stop boring.'

I note your plea. But to return to our theme, reactive action is compulsive behaviour, arising from the past. It comes from undealt with feelings inside us. Something triggers us and before we know it, we're out of control and reacting.

I'm familiar with that.

Reactive action tends to be self-justifying, self-serving, frightened, angry and on a bad day describes much of our behaviour.

Not a pleasant thought.

But responsive action is a very pleasant thought. This action is considered behaviour arising from present awareness. It comes from a place inside us where feelings are acknowledged but not worshipped.

Acknowledged but not worshipped? That can be a hard line to draw.

True. But this is the place from where much of our action would come if we took twenty seconds before reacting.

Good rule.

It's also the place we would speak from if we left the place of conflict, wherever it is, and took a short walk to acknowledge the strong feelings coursing through our body.

They can surge, can't they!

And it's is the place from where almost all our behaviour can arise from if we learn solitude.

*

How does solitude change things?

In solitude, we re-connect with humanity.

You mean we sometimes lose that connection?

In solitude we remember again what we share with those who we deal with and act upon.

The popular assumption is that people who like solitude don't like people.

Popular assumptions are usually wrong and this one is no exception. A true solitary is not one whose withdrawal isolates them from people. A true solitary is one whose aloneness builds bridges with people – bridges which perhaps action has left broken or wobbly.

I have a few wobbly bridges myself at present.

With bridges rebuilt and communion restored, we return to action more likely to respond rather than react.

It's just my fear of people.

Solitude calms our fears. While loneliness encourages our fear of people, solitude dissolves it and that makes a difference. As you have observed, it's our frightened selves that so often get reactive.

*

You mentioned two gifts of solitude at the start.

You were listening.

It's easy to listen at the beginning. So what's the second gift?

The second gift is this: darkness.

Darkness?

We remember that sometimes it's good to switch out the light and sit in darkness.

Why?

It reminds us of something important about ourselves.

And what's that?

It reminds us that we don't need to borrow someone else's light.

But what if we like their light?

Our love of light forms our habit. Our habit is to switch on the light when we enter a room and demand the electricity does the work.

Not a crime.

On other occasions, we ask others to be the light for us and bask in the reflected glory of their actions. 'Oh, don't worry – Sally will do it. She's brilliant! We can just sit back and enjoy!'

So you want us to sit in darkness?

Alone in the quiet darkness, we're reminded that ultimately, we are the light and that we are all we have. We can borrow light all our lives, whether by flicking the switch or relying on others, but the only true light we have is the light within ourselves. It's this light we engage with in solitude and then take out into the world.

✻

What we do in life echoes in eternity, as Maximus reminds us in the film *Gladiator.*

And more pressingly, it echoes down our street and in our office.

True. So we return to where we started: in solitude, we look after our actions and they do need looking after.

Through our actions, we impregnate the world.

21. Now

How can I arrive in the present?

'You do not need to leave your room,' writes Franz Kafka. 'Remain sitting at your table and listen. Do not even listen, simply wait. Do not even wait, be quite still and solitary. The world will freely offer itself to you to be unmasked. It has no choice. It will roll in ecstasy at your feet.'

That sounds like a path to the present.

✳

Arriving in the present is not easy.

True.

It's not easy because we spend most of our time in the past or the future.

Somehow they feel more real.

But this habit doesn't bring happiness and is a sure sign that we're giving our head unfortunate dominance in our lives at the expense of our senses.

How do you mean?

When touching a piece of pottery or sniffing the chill air of an autumn morning, I am in the present.

OK.

But regretting past mistakes I am not. Neither am I present when I'm feeling guilty or recalling some success or clinging to resentment over injury done to me - these are past things.

They can consume our time.

And neither am I present when I'm projecting forward. I'm not present when I'm thinking of events to come or dreading an outcome or imagining everything will be better round the next corner - these are future things.

My mind finds it hard to stay in the present.

And we shouldn't be surprised. The random collection of thoughts that is our mind has no anchor in the present. So while our search for the present can start in the mind it must soon leave there for the senses of touch, sight, sound, taste and smell – these, like our breathing, are always present.

So smelling a flower is a present thing?

This sense of smell is now; It knows no other place to be. Welcome to the present.

*

It's hard not living in the past, because it's always with us. Any suggestions?

In approaching our past, whether with relish or rage, the genius is a lightness of touch. There's nothing wrong with saying 'Remember when..!' and recounting the incident. If it was fun it can all be very merry and full of laughter.

And if our memories are unhappy?

If they're unhappy, then it can be healing to talk.

But we consider both sets of memories with an increasing lightness of touch for they no longer define us. The good old days and the bad old days – or more probably, the good/bad old days – have slipped like sand through our fingers and now offer us neither a home nor a prison.

And the future?

The future also requires a lightness of touch. I remember as a priest having to fill in funding forms from grant making bodies. They would ask for projections of where we wanted to be in one year, two years, three years, five years even.

Which all felt a bit mad?

I was struck by the imaginary and therefore ridiculous nature of the exercise. For something that did not exist, we were being asked to take the future very seriously. It's absurd to take the future seriously.

No organisation can know where there'll be in three or five years - too many imponderables.

I agree. But these grant-making bodies were only doing what everyone does when they spend time imagining a future, good or bad.

*

Any more handy hints about staying present?

It's often tension that keeps us from the present and tension emanates from the mind. So having a hot or cold bath or shower might help. The heat will relax and the cold will shock the tension away. I jumped into a freezing cold river recently which rendered me very present.

Hot bath for me.

Exercise leading to physical exhaustion is also good for tension, as is becoming aware of our breathing. As we know, our breathing is always present and takes us into our body and away from our mind.

Noted. And if that doesn't help?

It's about our intent; our intent to move beyond the tricks the mind plays on the body. It may be that in the time available we get no further than noticing the tension that lodges itself in our body. That's a start – at least we're in touch with something present.

I suppose so.

But in the long term, we don't want tension lodging in our body; we want it passing through our body. So more profoundly, if we're tense, we need to ask why it is so. Who or what has such power to keep us from the only place where we truly exist - which is now. If we have given someone the keys to our moods, then we need to take the keys back from them.

No one need have a set of those keys?

No.

*

In the meantime, we rejoin Kafka at his eternal table, listening: 'Do not even listen, simply wait. Do not even wait, be quite still and solitary. The world will freely offer itself to you to be unmasked.'

22. When everything's bad

What happens when our cracks begin to show?

Speaking generally, solitude is less something we do and more something that comes and finds us. It calls out for us in the tangled forest of life: 'Are you there?' Whether we answer the call or choose to hurry on is up to us.

I don't always answer the call.

Maybe not, but something in you is now answering otherwise you wouldn't be here.

True.

So the question is: where will the path of solitude take you today?

*

In this chapter, we reflect on dark times; times when everything seems bad.

They come, don't they?

They do yes, though surprisingly, not everyone thinks that's a bad thing.

'I like people to be unhappy,' says Virginia Woolf, 'because I like them to have souls. We all have, doubtless, but I like the suffering soul

102

which confesses itself. I distrust this hard, this shiny, this enamelled content.'

So she believed suffering made people more human, less hard. I can see a truth there.

Yes. Her words are hardly cheering for those in the valley of despair but they do ask questions of us.

Like what?

Well, like Humpty-Dumpty, we don't enjoy falling off the wall and we don't appreciate our cracks. But is it possible they're letting in some light through the enamel?

I suppose it depends on how we react and what resources we can muster in ourselves.

True. There's nothing good in suffering if we're unable to use it.

*

What's a positive here?

I'll give you a positive. When we're in trouble, solitude is eager to make contact.

Really?

Very eager. But many of us are inclined to ignore it because when we're in trouble, everything else seems more important.

Go away! Leave me to my disaster! Woe is me! I am not worthy!

That's right. Or our inner voice might say something like this: 'My house is too messy for a visit from solitude. Solitude only likes clean houses, good houses, happy houses! What can it do for me now I'm so down? These are hard times not holy times!'

Hard times not holy times? That sounds like a dangerous separation.

It is but thoughts like these may pass through our mistaken minds.

And the alternative?

If we open the door and allow solitude to enter, she begins to reshape things and it's best if we don't interfere. Instead, we allow her to do her work. As the Zenrin poem has it:

Sitting quietly, doing nothing
spring comes, and the grass
grows by itself.

*

As solitude begins her work there may be intruders.

What sort of intruders?

When everything is bad, our old voices speak. They are recognised by their anxious, fearful and despairing tones. And again and again, we listen to their counsels of hostility, hopelessness and self-pity.

They can be convincing.

Indeed. So we declare ourselves bitter or declare ourselves victims or whatever. These ghost voices of our personality have always been our default position when stressed and now they speak their dull lines again.

I can feel the pity-party getting underway.

But before it does, let's pause and listen.

Listen for what?

Let us listen out not for the ghost voices of our personality but for vibrant voices of our essence, our essential selves, for these speak of quite different things and speak more truly.

Can you hear them?

I'm not sure.

They may be faint but they're there. Is there anything apart from anxiety and despair in you?

I need time.

The existence of these other voices may surprise you. But with their arrival on the scene, balance is restored. Now anxiety is met by in-anxiety, fear by un-fear and despair by non-despair.

It's faint but I think I can sense other voices.

*

When we listen like this, we're experiencing a conversation inside ourselves between two very different sets of voices.

How long does it go on for?

It continues until the ghost voices slink off into the shadows, aware they no longer have the power they once enjoyed.

They'll return, of course. They'll return when we're stressed, just as they have always done. And who knows, perhaps they will sound convincing again.

But we listen to other voices now?

Yes, when the negative sirens return, our true voices, nurtured in solitude, will be there. They will meet with them again and speak with them again, in-anxious, un-fearful, non-despairing.

*

When everything's bad, we don't look away from the badness.

Which is sometimes tempting.

Instead, we look through it to something beyond. This is what Rabindranath Tagore suggests:

'The cure for all the illness of life is stored in the inner depth of life itself, the access to which becomes possible when we are alone. This solitude is a world in itself, full of wonders and resources unthought of.'

I like the idea that the cure for life is stored in life itself, in where we are now. In the substance of our present life is both the problem and the solution. We just need to access it?

That's the work. In solitude, badness becomes transparent instead of opaque; we begin to see through it as when sun burns away the cloud.

Badness, like solid cloud, looks and feels like the end of the story but it never is the end of the story?

And so when everything's bad, you push back the foliage and take the path of solitude. You may have strength for nothing else, but that's all right.

The path itself is your strength.

23. Regret

How does today feel?

We have passed through many ages and turned so many pages to find our book of life open at where it is today.

Does it feel like a good page?

*

Some chapters of our lives we remember better than others.

True.

I was talking to an elderly lady who appears elsewhere in this book. Her name is Georgie and she can recall the day 70 years ago when she was evacuated from London during the war. As a three-year-old she was sent to a new home in Hitchin. She remembers every item of clothing she was wearing that day, and the fact that when she went in the house, she was the same height as the table. We have a remarkable capacity to remember certain things.

I can still remember the name of my friend in nursery.

But we also have a remarkable capacity to forget things or bury things way beyond remembering.

Memory is selective, isn't it?

And often with good reason. These memories are hard to recover even if we wish it and often we don't. They were buried for a reason and nothing in us desires to see them dug up.

I suppose such forgetfulness does tell its own story.

And this brings suffering. Even if we cannot see the memories, we still hold them in our body like old stains on a cloth. Our mind may not remember everything but our body does and the shock waves still pass through us. As Virginia Woolf once wrote in her diary: 'If I had time to prove it, the truth of one's sensations lies not in the fact but in the reverberations.'

What had happened to her?

She had been sexually abused by her two half-brothers. It was never acknowledged and caused her mental health problems for the rest of her life.

So how do you deal with your regrets?

*

Regret can keep us from the experience of solitude. Not wishing to sit in the company of regret, we try to put it all behind us and move busily on.

It's the voice of the age. We're always being told to 'Just move on!'

So we shun solitude, preferring the frenetic pretence of some activity or other; and this is a shame, both for ourselves and the universe.

We're frightened people, people on the run.

And what we're most frightened of is the truth.

Are you serious?

People claim they want the truth but this is rarely the case. We resist it with a passion.

But that's mad.

It may be mad but is also understandable. In order to survive as children, we had to cover up a great deal, particularly our feelings - and we've taken this habit into adult life. Anything which now serves to uncover these things will return us to childhood fears and make us very uncomfortable.

So solitude can appear threatening?

Solitude is a great truth-teller, yes. But maybe now is the time to embrace this rather than run from it.

The time when we finally find the strength not to be scared?

Why be afraid when the truth sets us free? And why do we imagine the prison of untruth is such a fine place? In my experience, it's rather a wretched place.

*

But isn't regret forever?

If held gently, regret dissolves in the light of a particular truth.

And what truth is that?

The truth that we do what we are able to do.

How do you mean?

This is how it is. If we could have done more in the past, we would have done more and this is true for others too. We do what is possible for us in the moment. We take responsibility for what we do and live the consequences. But that is different from the netherworld of regret which is closely related to self-indulgence and self-pity.

There's something hopeful there.

Something profoundly hopeful. In solitude, we trace the rainbow through the rain. We acknowledge that we're not in control of our lives;

that we never have been and never will be. Instead, we know ourselves to be part of a world of precarious adjustment to the moment.

Meaning?

As in a conversation with friends, we adjust constantly to the mood and direction of the talk and so it is with our lives. Regret is for those who imagine they are in control.

People who say 'I could have done something about it.'?

When in fact they couldn't because we -

- do what we are able to do.

In solitude, we loosen our grip on control and find ourselves in a listening place. Here we become tender with ourselves and more engaged with life now.

*

And we become less blind, more seeing.

More seeing? How do you mean?

Sometimes regret blinds us to all the good things that are growing around us. And believe me, they are many.

And maybe we stop punishing ourselves as well?

That's always a good idea. There's not a human who has lived who could not have done things differently. Everyone has their 'If only's' and if we had a mind to, we could load ourselves down with regret that would crush an ox.

But we don't?

Solitude is for holding each regret, each 'if only' and throwing them like a white dove into the air for their place is no longer with you.

We do what we are able to do, we learn as we go – sometimes slowly – and we trace the rainbow through the rain. Life has brought you to now and now is fine.

Now is fine?

Or as Dag Hammerskold said: 'For all that has been 'Thank you'; for all that shall be, 'Yes''

24. Time

Is it possible to leave time behind?

'When everything has left you, you are alone; when you have left everything behind, there is solitude.'

Who said that?

Freidrich Schiller in his song, *Solitude.* Alone is when things leave you. Solitude is when you leave things and that includes time.

Time? How can you leave time?

*

In solitude, we submit to a different time scale. We disengage from our familiar chronology in which time presses upon us. We need a different chronology here.

That sounds like a big adjustment.

Maybe. We're used to things being instant. We fume as we wait a few minutes for a bus or a few seconds for an internet connection. And whereas in the old days if you wanted a book, you planned a trip to the library later in the week, today you can have an e book in your hand in 30 seconds without having to take off your slippers.

I'm terrible at waiting.

Then consider 1066, the last time Britain was successfully invaded by a foreign power. It took many Britons over a year to realise there had been a battle, that they had a new king and that he was called William. Did the wait make them unhappy? Did it in any way change the quality of their lives?

Probably not.

Today we'd insist on live coverage of the Battle of Hastings. We wouldn't wait a year for news of the outcome; we wouldn't have to wait a second.

But normal time still matters.

We need to get to work on time; punctuality is a practical kindness and let there be kindness in everything. But beneath the daily demands, we need to nurture a new sense of time. In solitude the rules are different: time is different, success is different.

How?

Here there are no deadlines for there is nothing to be delivered and no pressure to achieve because there is no target. You cannot race towards a line if there is no line.

Sounds like a charter for the lazy!

Then you're not seeing it well and calling an eagle a duck. Such an adjustment is for the brave not the lazy. The lazy don't actively adjust; they passively drift.

Point taken.

So the lazy won't find this hard. They'll simply find ways to avoid it. But others will find it hard.

Who like?

The time-conscious.

Why will they find it hard?

They wish to use every second well and get something worthwhile from every moment. So solitude may prove frustrating.

How do you mean?

If these people go on a day-conference, they bring away a resource manual and perhaps a certificate. They can say 'This is what I got out of it!'

But solitude? There's no certificate or paper qualification here. 'What exactly am I going to get from it?' they'll ask. 'If I'm to give time to solitude, what's the pay-off? I don't like wasting time.'

None of us want to waste time.

✳

Permit me a memory.

The privilege of the old.

I remember when I looked after a community centre in London's West End. It included a day centre for the elderly. Various activities would be arranged for them and I particularly recall Lucy and the candle maker.

Sounds interesting.

The candle maker had brought his gear to help them make their own candles. He stood over his tub of molten wax and explained to the participants how to go about it. Each was given a wick and they were to dip their wick into the hot wax and then quickly withdraw it. They should then allow the wax to cool, before dipping it in again. This way, layer upon layer of wax gradually built up around the wick, which in time became the candle.

What could possibly go wrong?

Lucy. She was an impatient soul who did not want the candle making to take up too much time. She did not want to waste time. She wanted her candle as quickly as possible and so decided on a short cut to glory.

Instead of quickly withdrawing the wick from the molten wax as advised, she held it in for longer in order to gain more wax and therefore speed up the process.

I see a problem.

Yes. Her impatience gave her the opposite of what she desired. The longer she held the wick in the hot wax, the more the wax on her wick melted. After 25 minutes, when the others were celebrating their home-made candles, a frustrated Lucy had barely anything to show.

She was angry with everyone except herself and called it 'a big waste of time'. But it was Lucy's attitude to time that had worked against her.

So what is your relationship with time?

*

Time is an elusive and unpredictable companion. Sometimes it whips us along at breathtaking pace, passing like the speed of light. At other times, it moves as slow as a slug in treacle, inching painfully forward.

And some say we're all caught up in just one moment?

That's right. Their view is that time is not a line of many moments but just one moment, the eternal moment. There is only the big now, pulled and stretched into different shapes, scenes and eras.

I can feel some truth there.

Certainly there's an eternity of time passing through us, like a wick through a candle; and it's this eternity, this ancientness of time that we connect with in solitude rather than the pressed and urgent variety. We may only have ten minutes to spare; but it's ten minutes lived by the clock of eternity on which the only time is the ancient, present and future now.

What is it they say? 'Nothing can be loved or known in haste.'

Indeed. So we allow our solitude to be slow today. Our watch can do punctuality but not eternity.

25. Therapy

Who helps you?

We all need therapy and have all experienced therapy.

Not me.

I'm talking about all sorts - paid or unpaid, formal or informal.

Well, obviously I've been helped by chatting to someone occasionally.

We're all therapists to someone and the word comes from the Greek word *therapeia*, meaning 'attendance'; someone attending on another.

I didn't know that.

This developed into meaning the treatment which the one in attendance administered. Friends are sometimes our best therapists and some swear by their hairdressers. At other times, a professional feels like a better option.

So the question is: who helps you? Have you had good experiences or bad experiences of 'attendance'?

*

It might be interesting to have some real life stories from therapy.

I could do that.

It would help de-mystify it.

Fair enough, let's try that. But the two stories I tell I choose not because they're startling but because they're entirely normal.

Just so long as they're true.

OK but we'll change the names and one or two particulars to ensure confidentiality. So meet Christopher who is reading me some very aggressive texts from his partner.

You're describing the session?

I am, yes. And in these texts, she calls him all the negative names under the sun.

Things are not well?

Christopher then tells me that such abuse is quite normal; that she puts him down all the time and tells him that their relationship can only continue if he improves.

What was she doing?

The message seemed to be this: 'You are sick, Christopher and I am trying to save you. Be grateful.'

How did Christopher feel about this?

You might be surprised to hear that he was very grateful and in awe of her wonderful kindness.

Was that your understanding?

No, from where I sat, the relationship was killing him. His partner was no saviour; indeed she was probably sicker than he was. He had a issue with pornography but salvation for Christopher lay in himself rather than in infantile dependency on a brittle and controlling partner.

He remained sure that he was not worthy of her. But before leaving, he added one thing: 'She's always demanding I say sorry. But she has never said sorry. Never.'

How do you react to that story?

I suppose it made her feel good to be saving someone. It seems she had to feel superior to him. Doesn't sound like a very healthy connection either way.

*

And when you're ready, we're going to meet Jasmine.

Someone entirely different?

Yes. She's telling me about her wonderfully close relationship with her eldest son. She speaks passionately about the special bond between them.

So a happy story?

But what soon becomes apparent is this: her 'wonderful' relationship with her son is all about her needs.

Ah.

She does not get on with her husband, finds no support there and has transferred her dependency needs to her eldest son.

Whether he wants them or not.

Now aged 19, he will have to leave home, both physically and emotionally, before he can come to his own understanding of a relationship which has so enveloped him from his early years. And Jasmine must let him go.

Will she have the courage?

I hope so.

But it's like asking someone to let go of a life raft in the sea.

True. The difference being that you need a life raft in the sea, but she does not need this relationship as it currently exists. It's not helpful for her.

*

People's experience of professional therapy varies. It can be all things from helpful and healing to damaging and dangerous. Therapy is about the attendance of another; but not all attendance is helpful.

So why do unhelpful things happen?

Sometimes it's the client who makes healing impossible. Perhaps they wish to be heard but not healed.

How do you mean?

They can be heard at no cost to themselves, but healing may well bring pain.

You mean they want to talk about their problems but they don't wish to consider why they might have them. I can identify with that.

So they play every game under the sun to avoid connecting again with that child who left so much behind to become an adult.

But it isn't always the client's fault.

No, sometimes the therapist makes healing impossible. Perhaps they worship at the shrine of their own wisdom and need the session to prove their professional competence. So they don't listen, believing they know it all already. But there's no healing without listening and no meeting of two people without listening.

Agreed.

Or perhaps placed above the client's needs is the therapist's need for a certain mystique or kudos, superiority even.

Yes, I can imagine that.

The gift of the good therapist is not to know more than us, but to bring to the surface what we know already but have lost sight of. We already know everything we need to know; but life has cut us off from our deep knowing, sometimes savagely.

*

Crucial to the therapeutic process is our use of solitude.

How so? Therapy is about two people isn't it?

It's good to talk and good not to talk.

Meaning?

Talking sometimes loosens things in our psyche that might otherwise have remained tight shut. Sometimes there is no substitute for talking. But it's also good not to talk, for new paths emerge as we reflect on our conversations with people. The greatest piano teacher in the world can do nothing for someone who does no practice alone; and the greatest therapist in the world can do nothing for someone unable to examine their life in solitude.

You mean listening back to the events of the day, for instance? Noting our feelings and reactions?

That's right. We get into all sorts of difficulties in life; this is normal. Shift occurs when we notice this instead of trying, like Christopher, to believe that all is as it should be. It helps no one to call someone a saviour when they're not a saviour; or in Jasmine's case, to call a relationship wonderful when it's clinging; or generally, to call something helpful when it's not helpful.

Isn't it best sometimes just to allow people their delusions?

I think I'm with Hafiz when he says:

'Love sometimes gets tired of speaking sweetly

And wants to rip to shreds
All your erroneous notions of truth . . .
The Beloved sometimes wants
To do us a great favour:
Hold us upside down
And shake all the nonsense out.'

Point taken!

Every therapist, professional or otherwise, has to gauge the moment when they stop speaking sweetly. It can make people very angry.

I suppose we're so immersed in things that it's hard to see the wood for the trees.

True. So in solitude, we withdraw from the battle, climb a hill and survey the scene of our lives. Maybe as we look, nothing is clear, so we just hold the scene before our eyes.

Or perhaps something is noticed with great clarity and a decision is born in us from our deep knowing.

It's your time now.

26. Space

Do you like to step into space?

People in relationships sometimes resent their partner wishing to be alone.

Oh, don't! Two of my best friends argue about this all the time. I stay out of it.

They imagine that if someone wishes to withdraw, it's a criticism of them or that they have offended in some way.

My friend definitely sees it as a criticism.

But far from damaging a relationship, solitude will almost always enrich.

How?

It creates a space in which the stresses and strains, the joys and the sorrows can be held. Without that space, significant dishonesty and manipulation will probably creep in.

I'm not going to be the one to tell them that.

✳

For Mirabel Osler, such space is the bringer of life. 'My idea of heaven,' she writes 'is opening a door into an empty room – not forever, I haven't enough resources, but for at least great chunks of time each day...a room or a garden, it doesn't matter which: vacancy is the breath of life.'

Vacancy as the breath of life? Most people like things full rather than empty.

Have you ever visited London's Tate Modern gallery?

Not my thing, really. You know it?

Their huge ground floor area on the south bank of the Thames hosts art installations and I've seen a few.

Any good?

Well, the truth is, I've never enjoyed a visit there quite so much as my last one when by chance, there was no display at all.

Nothing?

Nothing. The previous one had been removed, the next one was yet to arrive and in between we were left with no thing. It was strangely healing.

What was so healing about it?

It's hard to say. I suppose nothing there was trying to be clever and nothing was trying to make a point. The huge area was not trying to be anything other than what it was – space.

I found this invigorating because space is what we are made of and the space in the gallery called to the space within me.

I thought of Mirabel Osler's words.

*

I was thinking of the sculptor Anthony Gormley.

I can see why – many of his figures are set in mountainous areas where he believes the 'presence of distance' and closeness to the wind and sky removes us from our petty concerns and gives greater potential for consciousness.

And it's there that his figures can do their work?

That's his hope. 'Can the stillness and silence of the sculpture be a catalyst for stillness and silence?' he asks.

I know he fears the effects of the urban environment on people.

He's concerned about the absence of space and encourages city dwellers to 'try and find that other nature which maybe we've forgotten or maybe we've repressed.'

I'll be looking at his figures with new eyes now.

And then looking beyond; his passion is for them and their setting to remind us of our own spaciousness.

*

The word 'nirvana' is used by Buddhists to describe the attainment of heaven.

Yes, I think I knew that.

Literally, the word means 'a cooling off' or a 'going out', like a flame.

I didn't know that.

In Buddhist understanding, the flames that go out are the flames of craving, hatred and ignorance. And as these particular fires are extinguished and put to rest, there is a space left, hard to define but there in experience; it's a space beyond images and words and quite without boundaries.

Heaven available in our being?

That is Buddha's claim and perhaps Jesus' claim too when he said, 'The kingdom of God is within you.'

They do both seem to be speaking of a special space inside us.

As Martin Laird writes, 'Our interiority is not a cramped space but a valley of spaciousness. Clouds of thoughts and feelings come and go. We can identify these clouds with precision but we no longer identify with them.'

So let me understand this: where there is a going out of the flames of craving, hatred and ignorance we become a valley of spaciousness through which events and feelings pass but where none can dominate?

Well summarised. Here is a space free of distress, hostility and affliction and therefore a harbour for us, a shelter and a refuge. It is a beyond place and quite inviolable.

*

Perhaps you're reading this sitting on a Scottish mountain or maybe in a cramped train or flat. Whatever your circumstances, and they do affect us, you are space; you are a valley of spaciousness and no less so for being in a train rather than on a mountain.

In solitude today you tend that space, removing the rubbish and clutter. You're like a park keeper on Sunday morning dealing with the excesses of Saturday night. Inner clutter diminishes us as humans.

And as we create inner space, so we become contemplatives.

And they are?

As the old adage says: Victim – life happens to me; Activist – life happens round me; Contemplative – life happens through me.

27. Media

How does the media relate to your solitude?

To survive and make a profit, the media must serve our needs. But today we consider which particular needs it is serving.

And we start with a question: how do you relate to the media?

I don't know. I never thought of it as a relationship. I mean, it's just there, isn't it?

*

This is what I see every morning. People get a free newspaper at the tube station and read a couple of stories as they wait for the train. They then read six more stories as they travel to work. On arrival, they leave the newspaper on the seat, for its job is done. It's distracted them for the necessary 20 minutes and now it's time to get on with the business of the day.

Fair enough, surely?

Stay watching. The stories will have varied from funny and sad to gossipy and tragic. They'll have taken the reader around the world, 40 seconds here, two minutes there and then a quick 20 seconds somewhere else. Can they remember any of the stories as they walk to the office? Probably not, but as I say, they're not there to be remembered. The stories are there to distract, to entertain and to fill that difficult 20 minute gap on the train.

Yes, even the story about the famine, which is shocking but what can you do? And you're getting off at the next stop anyway...

That all seems a bit harsh.

But is it true?

I suppose.

Or imagine a different scenario. Perhaps for another it's not a newspaper but the celebrity gossip magazine as they wait for the hairdresser to be ready. They read the big interview, a half-page piece on the dangers of sun beds but it's mainly bite-size chunks about the soap opera lives of the briefly famous. Is any of it true? You cannot be sure and in a way it doesn't matter. The magazine is just there to distract between your early arrival and your appointment time.

*

What's the issue here?

The issue is to understand our relationship with the media.

The restlessness of the news plugs into our own restlessness. And as we immerse ourselves in the dramas, reactions and latest developments in the lives of others, it's possible for the restless news to transfer its restlessness to our inner lives. Like travellers bombarded with choices, we lose our bearings and become victims of anxiety and unsettledness.

I'm not denying that. I'm just wondering if it matters. We all love information.

And our desire for information is amply fed but this is not a creature which needs feeding. Rather than stuffing our hunger for information, we should calm it. This is not a happy child within us and needs care but not over-feeding.

*

So where's solitude in all this?

Struggling! When something limits us to a surface response, it denies us solitude. It's not illegal but it is unhelpful.

Why?

Because something that keeps us on the surface also keeps us from ourselves. We become puppets of a lesser god – a mind-tugging god who wishes us to look briefly at everything and deeply at nothing; a flitting god who demands that the eyes of all worshippers jump and hop from one thing to another like a demented butterfly.

And so it is that we become scattered people rather than gathered people.

Let me understand: we are those who are scattered within rather than gathered within?

Yes. If someone were to come to our door they would only hear a chaos of voices inside.

*

What can we do?

It's what we can not do which will be more freeing.

Explain.

Sometimes, we will not pick up the newspaper or magazine; and sometimes we shall not surf the internet. We shall ignore the lesser god of distraction, however it presents itself to us. Staying in the moment, we listen to our breathing. We're not reading about the world but we're present to the world and therefore liable to discover rather more.

Solitude is a triumph of quality over quantity.

28. The simple life, the creative life

What is a simple life?

It is the simple life rather than the busy life that creates most profoundly in the world.

That's a rather bold assertion.

Do not be deceived. The simple life might appear active on the surface; but beneath the surface, simplicity is prior to activity. And this makes all the difference.

Can you say the same? Or does everything feel rather complicated at the moment and rather stressed?

*

I'm all for solitude but it's busy people who get things done.

The important question is: what do they get done? We know they're determinedly doing this, that and the other. But what is the quality of their work? Many are busy out of their own need to be busy and this brings its own darkness.

And solitude brings light?

Anthony Storr thought so. As he says: 'It appears that some development of the capacity to be alone is necessary if the brain is to function at its best and if the individual is to fulfil his highest potential.'

He's suggesting that the greatest acts and achievements arise out of an ability to be alone?

His words make me think of Gandhi who was a man who perhaps came near to fulfilling his highest potential. He was a busy human but also a simple human wedded to his solitude.

How was this expressed?

On his ashram, he would arise around three or four in the morning to take advantage of the cool and quiet of the Indian morning. He would do this even amid the most pressing national crises which were plentiful in his day.

It's easy on an ashram.

Maybe. But his seizure of solitude was not merely for the ashram. It was his daily habit wherever he was: whether on a train or in London for talks or while held in a prison cell. It was the most essential part of his day, more so than meals. Every morning he felt he was given energy which he drew from for the rest of the crowded day.

It was his solitude which made his life simple?

It was the sea of peace into which even the most turbulent rivers emptied themselves and were stilled.

*

Is this chapter just for creative people?

We're all creative people.

Really?

Undoubtedly. Sometimes the impression is given that only painters, musicians or fashion designers are creative; that these are the 'creative types' while the rest of us wade around in a lesser world of humdrum functionality.

I suppose I've always thought that.

Think it no longer because it's a grand gathering of nonsense. We're all creative people, creating both in what we do and more profoundly, through who we are.

An example?

The teacher who returns home after creating a climate of learning and discovery for a Year Nine physics class has created just as much as much as Picasso; while the supermarket manager who daily deals honourably with staff and customers alike is unquestionably on a par with Christian Dior's chief clothes designer.

Well, that's a different view!

Creativity is not about our ego or about making our mark on the world. Rather, it's about liberating ourselves and those around us into the present moment.

And solitude?

Solitude is the cradle of this child. Solitude gives us present definition, present awareness and this is creative energy. 'As we lose our vagueness about our self, our values, our life,' writes Julia Cameron, 'we become available to the moment. It is there, in the particular, that we contact the creative self. Until we experience the freedom of solitude, we cannot connect authentically. We may be enmeshed but we are not encountered.'

I like her distinction at the end between being enmeshed and being encountered. Enmeshed suggests being trapped; encountered suggests being alive.

*

We're all the creative types and our creativity is fed and deepened in aloneness and simplification. The other day I heard a modern artist speaking about this.

What was their view?

'It is essential to unclutter the brain,' says Gilbert from Gilbert and George: 'to live the simplest life possible and to encumber yourself with the fewest possible choices. If you do so, a clear creative desert lies open before you.'

They live in London's East End, don't they?

They do and in the cause of simplification, choose to travel as little as possible and eat in the same restaurant every day where they enjoy the same meal.

Wow!

With their income, they could have all sorts of adventures but that is not their choice. 'We don't want anything, we have everything,' they say.

*

We're reflecting on the relationship between the simple life and the creative life. Our tasks vary but we're all creative people.

I'm coming round to that idea.

When I left the priesthood and worked for three years in a supermarket, I never felt my creative days were done; my days were just different. I may have been less honoured but honour is a passing thing while our creativity is endless.

So how should I simplify my life?

By listening and by letting go. Allow those practices more space in your life.

*

'I have not the shadow of doubt,' writes Gandhi, 'that any man or woman can achieve what I have if he or she would make the same effort and cultivate the same faith and hope.'

He's talking about creative types like you.

Like me?

29. The Royal Court

Who has helped you down the years?

A long time ago, there was a king called Uss and he was accompanied by his entourage. This included his Bodyguard, his Jester, the Chief Counsellor, his Physician and the Head of the Household.

Lucky old Uss!

They all had their roles to play in his life. In a violent world, where assassins were only a knife thrust away, the bodyguard was there for his physical protection.

Crucial.

The jester was different. He would appear during the banquets to lighten proceedings and to remind the king to take himself and his power less seriously.

Sounds healthy.

The chief counsellor was his wise man who advised both on the grand affairs of state and on the king's personal behaviour which did need a careful eye.

Responsible job.

The physician was there for his physical well-being, someone who knew his body well, while the Head of Household organised the practical details of the court like the kitchens, the laundry and the ordering of candles.

And the point of this story?

The king's entourage contained various skills and gifts and each of us is a queen or a king with a similar court. In our lives, we surround ourselves with people who help us.

I suppose we do.

We've considered five people who were there for King Uss. So can you now name five people who in their different ways have been or are significant for you? What have they each given to you? What do they give to you?

*

In solitude we reflect on our own royal court down the years.

I've got my pen and paper out. I'm scribbling down names and remembering things I'd forgotten. Interesting.

People come and go. Some are there briefly but helpfully at a key moment in our life; others stay longer with a steady contribution.

I had a body guard at school, someone who looked out for me; and I certainly have a jester in my life at the moment. He makes me laugh but doesn't let me off the hook. He's dangerous to know in a way.

It's good to celebrate our court and to be thankful for these special people in our lives. Sometimes we can get negative and part of that negativity is to cut ourselves off from others, see ourselves as unloved and imagine it's us against the world.

Yes, that happens.

We're then inclined to forget how many angels have walked our path with us and still do.

*

Can we talk about the negative feelings? They struck a chord.

Negative feelings can be a defining factor in our lives without us realising it.

That's what I'm sensing.

It may be that you feel let down by your royal court; feel that it hasn't been very 'royal' at all.

Maybe.

Or perhaps you long for a court like that of King Uss but have never been given it: 'If only I'd had a Chief Counsellor!'

Or perhaps you simply feel betrayed.

There are a lot of feelings around.

It's helpful to notice what you feel you've lacked or still lack. These things do less damage when noticed.

I'll take your word for it.

But it's not helpful to turn such awareness into self-pity. Note what you have lacked and then note what you have. You may have lacked much down the years; but you have all that you need and what you don't have you don't need.

More trust required to swallow that statement.

The clammy staircase of negativity, which reframes everything as a problem, has taken you downwards before but doesn't exist in the present.

Neither does it exist in thanksgiving. There's always an arrow of thanksgiving to be shot into the dark sky and such beautiful arrows tend to attract others to our cause.

*

To return to King Uss, he would withdraw sometimes. There he was, surrounded by his retainers when suddenly he'd be gone.

Where to?

No one was sure where he went but he left the royal court behind, even his bodyguard.

The unexplained absence of the king caused a certain degree of panic amongst the courtiers: 'I wish he'd at least take an armed guard with him!' they'd say. But they learned that they had to let him go.

He had a secret place?

He did.

Where was it?

It was secret. And here the king closed the door on his kingdom, for while he was grateful for them all, he was dependent on none.

Interesting.

And there he would gather wood and light a fire.

In court, servants did this for him. But in his secret place, King Uss lit the fire himself as a reminder that ultimately, he must be his own warmth and light.

30. My body

Are you a good caretaker of your body?

A top football manager was being asked about the pressures of the job. 'First of all,' he said, 'it's much tougher at the bottom than the top. But really, as long as you have your bodily health, you have everything.'

I agree. Physical health is such a gift.

And sometimes in solitude, it's good to let your body speak, away from the advice of doctors, friends and the latest health article in the newspaper.

What's wrong with them?

Nothing. They all have their place but so do you with your own listening and your own reflections.

After all, you're the only one who lives in your body and so you're its caretaker and responsible for it.

I'm the caretaker. OK.

How does your body feel today? Are you in good relationship with it?

As its caretaker, are you taking care?

*

Like a river, our body is always changing.

How do you mean?

You never step into the same river twice and the body you live in today is not the body you lived in yesterday; things have changed. Perhaps you're making yourself thinner; perhaps you're allowing yourself fatter or maybe age is denying you things you once enjoyed.

I take your point.

And sometimes there is the shock of an accident or news of a serious condition. Our body is a soap opera of concerns. Sometimes we enjoy it and at other times, it feels like we're watching a tragedy.

I've had my moments.

Whatever our condition, our body is always telling us something, always reporting back. And so it's good to be in conversation with it. Perhaps as stillness settles, you celebrate your health and become aware that it's something you've rather taken for granted.

Endlessly.

We ask our body to do so many remarkable things each day and we do not always say thank you for the routine miracles it performs.

*

And remembering that both honesty and awareness are a feature of our solitude, it's possible we have a nagging fear or worry about our body.

How do you mean?

I know someone who sensed something was wrong inside them. She went to her doctor who suggested she was just depressed. She had to pay five visits before they agreed to a blood test. It transpired she had leukaemia.

Or it may be something else. Obesity is one way of showing our psychological hurt on the outside - but there are other ways in which our body takes the strain of our psychology. Is there a sense we're being careless about our body by looking the other way?

I suspect there's a lot of that about.

This isn't a helpful habit. A spirit which cuts off from reality is an ill spirit and our body needs to be heard rather than ignored.

*

So there's a relationship between our psychology and our body?

The relationship between our physical and psychological bodies is now well established.

An example?

Take back pain.

I know all about that.

Back pain might start with an accident, over-exertion or some other physical cause but the emotions are quickly involved.

How?

Presented with the pain in our back we begin to worry about the injury and fear further injury.

Worry and fear? Not a good combination.

The worry and the fear bring tension to the back muscles and cause further pain bringing further worry and fear.

*

That's all very well but isn't this a book about solitude?

In solitude we practice mindfulness.

Mindfulness?

Mindfulness is best defined as awareness of our present experience with acceptance.

You wrote a book about this?

One-Minute Mindfulness, yes, but that isn't for now. What we note is that in mindful solitude, we begin to change our relationship with pain.

How can you relate to something you don't want?

We start a conversation with it. We don't want the pain but we speak with it because it's part of who we are. In this way, some people come to a place of acceptance. And we cannot change anything until we accept it.

We travel different paths to this place and perhaps surprise ourselves along the way. And here we find ourselves free from the toxic emotions of worry, fear or despair which can accompany and worsen pain.

*

But healing is not all in the mind.

No, our body is both a robust and fragile chemical balance. I endured a few difficult years when unknown to me and unseen by anyone else, my pituitary gland stopped producing thyroxin with consequent effects. My doctor, incorrect in his diagnosis, told me to stop eating spicy foods which was not a help.

What were you thinking?

I just assumed I was getting old but my assumption was mistaken and my caretaking careless.

So what happened?

It was only by chance – if chance exists - that my condition was discovered; but discovered it was and I'm now the beneficiary of daily thyroxin tablets and the chemicals are doing their wonderful work.

Our psychology is soaked in chemicals and our chemicals soaked in psychology.

*

Perhaps I can be more aware of my body today.

In solitude, you could use the simple body meditation. Start with your feet and ankles and then move on to your shins, knees, thighs, groin and abdomen and so on until you reach your head. Pause for a moment in each place, allowing space for any feelings which need to appear.

A friend of mine does that in yoga.

Your friend could probably give you some help then. You're the caretaker of your body, so it's good to listen. Who knows? Your body might even ask questions of you.

31. Death

What is it we fear about death?

It is early morning in a hospital and a man sits with his dead mother. He has been there for an hour and a half, alone.

He wasn't sure when she finally stopped breathing but she's quite still now.

Doctors? Nurses?

He could have called the doctors and nurses to come and attend to her. But instead, he wished for solitude now the end had come. He had things to say to her, things to feel before the reaction of others filled the space.

Oh yes, that happens.

In time, he would look after them in their shock. But for now, there was too much sorting to be done with his own thoughts and feelings in need of attention.

Mixed feelings?

Some were warm thoughts, some were angry and frustrated but all needed time.

And so as the moon bid a faint goodbye and the sun rose on a new day, he sat in hospital solitude with death.

*

What is it we fear about death?

More than asking what we did, death asks us who we are; and some-times people fear death because they don't yet know who they are.

Surely there's something in them that would like to find out?

Oh yes, they'd love to know who they are. But amid the busyness of life, there just isn't the time, so everything is put on hold.

I think that's how it is with me, to be honest. Death remains awkward-ly in the shadows, like a meeting constantly postponed; the question of who I am can wait.

It's a theme taken up in the story of a woman at the gates of heaven. The angel at the gate has only one question: 'Who are you?' But the woman has some difficulty answering. She explains whose wife she is – some-one quite famous, actually – and also that she's a mother and a doctor and a leading light in the Amateur Dramatic Society where she sits on two committees.

But each time she offers one of these descriptions the angel is dissat-isfied and merely repeats the question: 'But who are you?' In the end, she's sent back to earth to discover who she is rather than the roles she plays.

*

Sometimes people are mourned for what they did. I remember a young mum particularly sad at the death of her aunt because 'she was a great babysitter.' It was a useful role now withdrawn and she was upset about that. This might appear a shallow response –

- just a bit -

- but understandable. If we define ourselves by what we do then it's hard not to see others in the same way.

Not everyone's like that.

No, others experience a deeper sense of loss when someone close or revered dies. It's not what the person did that is gone but who they were, their essence.

The world is now a different place. That's what I found.

They left without us and we must now live without them. Somehow we must find the resources to cope with our aloneness in this vast universe.

And if we're familiar with solitude it helps?

Of course. 'Solitude,' writes Thomas de Quincey, 'though it may be silent as light, is like light, the mightiest of agencies; for solitude is essential. All come into this world alone; all leave it alone.'

Perhaps that's why we fear solitude. It feels like a premonition of death.

If it does, then it's here that some of our fears can be calmed; for we have nothing to fear in solitude and nothing to fear in death.

*

We started in the early morning solitude of a hospital ward where a man sat contemplating the life and death of his mother. He could have called people to his side and opted for noisy and busy company; but for a while he chose the solitary way.

I hope I'd do the same.

In solitude, we invite the angel of death out of the shadows and find him surprisingly kind company. We put down what we do and consider who we are. And we put down what others do and consider who they are.

It is all strangely life-bringing.

32. Epiphany

Will solitude bring me joy?

'Silence is the perfectest herald of joy,' says Shakespeare and sometimes this is true.

Only sometimes?

We will experience many revelations in solitude and one of them may be joy. Or it may be something else – light comes in many different shades. This morning, for instance, I'm looking out my kitchen window and watching the day slowly dawn. Somehow the dawning becomes my own.

I like the idea of an inner light.

You remind me of a story told of El Greco, the Spanish painter. A friend visited him at home one day on a lovely spring afternoon. He found the artist sitting in his room with the curtains firmly drawn.

'Come out into the sunshine!' exclaimed his friend. 'It's wonderful!' 'Not now,' said the painter. 'It would destroy the light that is shining in me.'

*

An epiphany is a revelation.

I was wondering.

It's a moment when we see something in a new way, when scales fall off our eyes or where we are led into a new experience of insight, trust or joy.

I'd take any of those.

In the Buddhist tradition, the epiphany of Buddha under the bodhi tree is central.

Forgive my ignorance, but what actually happened?

Imagine the scene: Buddha is seeking enlightenment after many false attempts, including extreme asceticism. He'd punished his body and achieved nothing. But now he circles the bodhi tree until he finds 'the immoveable spot' and sits down.

He then makes this dramatic declaration: 'Let my skin and sinews and bones dry up, together with the flesh and blood of my body! I will welcome it! But I will not move from this spot until I have attained the supreme and final wisdom.'

And what happened?

He didn't – and he did.

I must buy a bodhi tree!

It's a powerful story but not one about a bodhi tree.

No?

Had sales of bodhi trees suddenly increased Buddha would have been sad. The bodhi tree was mythical, a symbol. He did not want people to obsess about the tree but about his psychological state.

Which state is that?

The state which allowed him to see the world and himself in perfect balance, in harmony.

The world and himself in perfect balance?

That's right. So this is a story not about the countryside but about our inner state. He didn't want people to attach themselves to the tree, but to their own discoveries.

We're to seek that balance and harmony for ourselves.

As a later follower famously said, 'If you meet Buddha along the way, kill him.'

Was he jealous?

No. He's simply making the point that our spirituality cannot be borrowed from others, however impressive they may be; it must be our journey driven by our seeking, our questions and our search.

✳

Don't Christians talk of epiphany?

In the Christian tradition, Epiphany Sunday celebrates the arrival in Bethlehem of the Three Kings, who had followed the star in search of the promised one.

I know the song: We Three Kings of Orient are!

Suddenly, as they arrive at the stable, they're gazing on the baby Jesus – it's an epiphany moment and they know their search is over.

So what are you searching for?

What am I searching for?

✳

We will not demand sensational news from our silence. Indeed, in silence we happily withdraw ourselves from the world's craving for the sensational and sit quietly in eternity. Here we are in cleaner air and as on a clear day, we can see for miles.

What do we see?

It will vary. Perhaps we notice only our reluctance to be here, our impatience to be somewhere else. This might particularly arise in the early moments.

It can be hard to settle.

Or maybe we experience a strange calm about something that previously troubled us.

Seized by a great calm! I've known that.

Or perhaps it's the opposite. We become suddenly unsettled as unbidden, an old scene replays itself again and again in our mind.

Again, familiar.

Sometimes a word is given. One woman recently told me how she was given three words so forcefully whilst driving alone that she had to pull over in the car. 'Was that God?' she asked.

What did you say?

I said if it wasn't, it was a pretty good imitation of him.

※

'When man sits,' writes Meister Eckhart, 'then the course passions subside and the luminous mind arises in awareness: thus conscience is illuminated.'

The course passions can hang around for a while.

That's true. What we notice is that there are no rules in solitude and we cannot control the outcomes. Buddha had struggled for a long time before his moment beneath the tree; and then a woman is given something beautiful and significant as she drives her car.

It does all appear a bit random.

Sometimes we're surprised by joy; at other times, we notice only our concerns, our present obsessions.

I suppose even that is an epiphany of a sort – and there I am, using the word for myself!

I agree. In solitude 'everything is material' as the therapists say, for we're now honest people open to seeing and fearless of seeing. We're content to walk in the shadow and the light and greet both as our friends with something to reveal.

It's time we pushed back the foliage and stepped onto the path. And before I leave, there's one simple practice that's always been helpful for me.

What's that?

Name your problem or question in the evening.

OK.

And look for the answers in the morning, open to all creation. We are found in strange ways.

33. The world

Does the world need my solitude?

We live in the world rather than a bubble and it's a world of terror, beauty, pain, courage, fear and delight. Here we meet hard hearts and big hearts, cold hearts and kind hearts, sometimes all in one day and sometimes all in one person.

How does your world feel today?

*

Life in the world is change.

Change is the only constant, as they say.

Day by day we negotiate, adjust, struggle and triumph.

But not necessarily in that order.

True. Sometimes it feels bad, sometimes it feels good and sometimes our feelings are so buried that we cannot feel anything. We're immersed in the world like a swimmer in the sea, buffeted by the waves, carried by the currents and part of a great stirring of which we understand but a little.

So what do we do?

The only thing we can do is to swim on, half-knowing but whole-hearted.

But where are we swimming to?

We make our way towards horizons we can glimpse but never comprehend.

And this is OK?

This is quite OK. The world needs us to do what we do. How much poorer the world would be if you did not do what you do.

It doesn't always feel like that.

But remember this: the world needs us as humans and not machines.

Meaning?

The world asks that we acquire a certain independence of spirit as we immerse ourselves in the crowd.

Why?

Because the crowd can be a hypnotic force whose mad rules can quickly become our own.

As Hafiz puts it:
'Listen: this world is the lunatic's sphere,
Don't always agree it's real,
Even with my feet upon it
And the postman knowing my door
My address is somewhere else.'

*

So although the world finds solitude cranky, the world desperately needs it. Solitude keeps our address 'somewhere else'?

Solitude keeps the world sane. Thomas Merton puts it well: 'In actual fact,' he says, 'society depends for its existence on the inviolable personal solitude of its members. Society, to merit its name, must be made up not of members or mechanical units, but of persons. To be a person implies responsibility and freedom and both these imply a certain interior solitude, a sense of personal integrity, a sense of one's own reality and of one's ability to give to society – or to refuse that gift.'

I didn't realise that to be a person was quite such a revolution.

*

The story of the laboratory frog must helpfully haunt every generation.

I know this one.

This is the frog who when dropped into boiling water leaps out to save its life. But also the frog who when put in cold water and warmed slowly does not notice the gradual change. As the water heats, the frog adjusts and adjusts and adjusts until it is too late.

He dies.

He does and those familiar with history know this already: we're rarely aware of the discreet but corrosive power of our own surroundings.

We think we're fine and everyone else is mad?

Every culture has looked askance on other cultures and found them at best intriguing and at worst laughable or evil. Every culture imagines it has the right to look over its proud shoulder and judge - blind to its own seething mass of absurdities.

Strong words.

And cultures are just individuals writ large. What cultures do, me and my neighbor do. We really believe that we're on the side of sanity in a way that others are not.

Why is that?

It's how we are and the most insane among us believe it the most. This explains the savagely comic story Jesus told of the person with a log in their eye. Do you know it?

Remind me.

The figure with the log in their eye, far from trying to mend themselves, is saying 'tut, tut!' to their friend who has a speck of dust in his eye. Displaying a marvellous lack of self-knowledge, the man with the log in his eye is desperate to remove the speck of dust in his friend's eye.

Jesus' advice?

Remove the log from your own eye first. Then you'll be able to see better to help your friend.

*

Perhaps every time of quiet should start with the words: 'I am a beginner, I know nothing and judge no one.'

Good idea. And this is why the world needs people of solitude. The world needs people who are putting distance between themselves and themselves and between themselves and the society in which they live. As we become aware of the voices inside us, we're better able to hear the shouts and commands of the world outside us.

How do you mean?

Well, we may find an external voice very appealing; but then we realise it's only appealing to something inside us that is not healthy. It has a negative appeal and that's never a helpful path to pursue.

So we become more able to discern which external voices we wish to salute and which we do not?

That's right - persons rather than machines. 'Be in the world but not of it', we are told in the Christian gospels, not because we are too good for the world but because the world needs us sane.

And in a way, we're back with the desert hermits.

Yes the desert hermits of the 4th century left the cities of their birth because it was the only sane thing they could do. They stepped into the solitude of the desert to recover themselves as people and to save themselves from the slow but deadly fate of the laboratory frog.

*

To live in the world and to serve the world we must learn sometimes to leave the world.

As Cardinal Basil Hume says, 'We shall never be safe in the market place unless we are at home in the desert.'

And you could walk into the desert now.

34. Battered

Why am I brought so low?

'And silence, like a poultice, comes to heal the blows of sound,' writes Oliver Wendell Holmes.

So if you're feeling battered today, perhaps you've come to the right place.

On behalf of silence, welcome.

*

We each know the blows of sound well.

I know them very well; particularly the sound of other people's cruel or thoughtless words.

Sometimes we can shrug them off as nothing, but at other times they leave their bruising mark.

So why does sound leave us so battered?

*

Here's a story about Jessica and her red coat.

I'm listening.

Jessica walks down the road in her new red coat. She's very proud of it.

'Who does the red coat belong to, miss?' ask some children.

'The coat belongs to me,' she says and is most upset when they run off laughing.

Further down the road she meets a girl.

'Who does the red coat belong to, miss?' she asks.

'The coat belongs to me,' she replies. Jessica can see from the girl's face that she wished she owned such a coat. This makes Jessica feel rather special.

Later, Jessica is buying some shoes when the manager asks about the coat.

'Who does the red coat belong to, madam?'

'The coat belongs to me,' says Jessica.

'You do know that it's last year's colour?'

Jessica is absolutely furious, incandescent with rage and storms out of the shop oblivious to everything but her sense of shame. Good riddance to that shop!

And she doesn't recover until she sits down for a cup of tea in a café across the road.

'Who does the red coat belong to, miss?' asks the waitress who then declares she's never seen such a fine coat.

'The coat belongs to me,' says Jessica who could not have been more delighted.

✱

One of the reasons we're so battered by life is our ego's possessive nature.

Expressed in what way?

It's the possessive nature which loves to say 'This belongs to me'. Whether it's a sun bed by the hotel pool or a particular role we play or our reputation, we love to say 'Mine!'

Which presumably was Jessica's problem?

Like a boat without stabilisers, she went from being absurdly crushed by negative comment to absurdly elated with a compliment.

A roller-coaster ride.

And all caused by her sense of ownership of the coat.

You mean, had it belonged to a friend, it would have been different?

Oh yes, completely different. You can hear her now , handing it back to its owner: 'Rather mixed reactions to your coat today, Barbera. Still, not to worry, eh? It's only a coat!'

But because she saw the coat as her possession, as part of her, it was a different story. And authors know this well. If we're unduly pleased with a good review, we can be equally sure we'll be devastated by a bad one.

So health for a writer?

Health for a writer is this: when something is written it's given away with a life of its own and in no sense possessed. Pick up this book and it's yours for a while; it hasn't been mine for a long time.

*

Like a monkey swinging through trees, our ego works through our mind, and so we'll be aware of our mind in solitude and help it as we can.

How can we help our mind?

Our mind is like a candle flame: unstable, flickering and entirely at the mercy of the conditions around it.

How do you mean?

With a candle, it's less about the flame itself and more about the air around the flame.

I see.

If the air is turbulent, the flame is vulnerable. But if we bring calm to the surrounding air, then the flame will burn still and bright.

And we can bring calm to our mental surroundings?

We can try. Sometimes it can be done by saying something simple like: 'I put down my claim. This doesn't belong to me.'

This allows our mind to stop being anxious and become a still flame again.

*

'Solitude is for me a fount of healing which makes my life worth living,' said the psychiatrist CG Jung.

You used that quotation earlier and I was trying then to imagine what he might mean.

You should have said.

It didn't feel important enough, and anyway, it's come round again.

Things tend to do that and often they come round again when we're ready for them. So what did he mean? I can't be sure. But perhaps in his treasured times alone Jung gave up ownership of his clients' health and of his famous therapeutic expertise. Freedom!

So psychiatrists can be quite as possessive as authors and women with red coats?

We'll allow everyone their darkness and seek the silence. Here is a poultice that can heal the blows of sound.

35. Still

How do I quieten my mind?

'To a mind that is still,
The whole world surrenders,'
Chuang Tzu.

That's a challenging start. A still mind is not easily achieved.

True. Sometimes, despite being away from people, we still find ourselves in dispute with them. We relive in our minds conversations we've had or imagine words we might speak next time we meet.

I get caught up in all that. It's infuriating!

We'll not punish ourselves for this, as there is no gain in that. But neither will we applaud or encourage ourselves in the activity.

I can generate a fair amount of self-righteousness in a matter of seconds.

Precisely. We merely notice what our mind is doing and notice the fears it's acting out. Why is this particular dispute, person or incident so obsessing me at present?

*

Stilling the mind can be like trying to catch a fly with tweezers. But strangely, stillness is best achieved if we do not seek stillness.

I beg your pardon?

I know it sounds odd but that doesn't make it untrue.

It does in my book.

I remember when young being told that if I had to walk down a road with no pavement, always to walk towards the oncoming traffic. This seemed like a death-wish at the time, complete madness; but there was sense there. It meant I could see the cars that were closest to me, the ones which would require me to move.

And your point is?

We're not always good judges of the truth. Our perceptions sort through the wheat and the chaff and frequently choose the chaff. And so we open ourselves to this strange possibility: that when we seek stillness it's best not to seek stillness.

OK, but why do you say that?

Those who seek stillness as the ultimate good may end up in a trance-like state similar to self-hypnosis. This can easily become an exercise in escapism, repression and denial. I see a lot of this - unhealth posing as health; something manufactured rather than natural.

So if we don't seek stillness, what do we seek?

We seek awareness – awareness of all the thoughts and feelings passing through us. If we seek awareness, stillness will take care of itself and when it settles, will be something natural rather than manufactured.

*

So the silence will be giving us messages?

'Every moment there is news coming out of silence,' writes Rainer Maria Rilke and he's right. Our developing genius for stillness will be seen in how we treat this news.

Like those disputes that carry on inside my head when I'm alone.

Yes, that's an example of news coming out of silence. So we notice these things, whatever they are and we allow them to come and then allow them to go.

I see.

What we don't do is welcome them in, give them a medal, cook them a huge meal and insist they stay for as long as they want!

Instead, we say 'Thank you for coming and thank you for going.'

You're getting the idea.

*

And we'll be patient with ourselves.

Not easy.

No, but the fact is, we are as we are for a reason. It's unlikely, for instance, that we were taught the pathway to stillness when young; indeed, it's likely we were encouraged along every pathway except this one. Standing Bear gives us some clues as to how we might proceed.

You've quoted him before.

I'm aware of that, but repetition is no bad thing. Solitude is not about acquiring information but using information. The first time we hear something, we appreciate it on one level; the second time we hear something, we appreciate it on another level. The second time is more use.

As the Steve Turner poem has it:
  'History repeats itself.
  Has to.
  Nobody listens.'

So the quote?

'Training began with children who were taught to sit still and enjoy it. They were taught to use their organs of smell, to look where there was apparently nothing to see and to listen intently when all seemingly was quiet. A child who cannot sit still is a half-developed child.'

＊

When young, most of us were taught the active and busy paths rather than the still and listening paths.

Nothing's changed. Some parents work their socks off to keep their children entertained and away from silence.

True. If they're not driving them to an activity they're putting a computer in their bedroom. Half-developed children breed more half-developed children. Afraid of solitude themselves adults pass their fear onto their children. It creates people with few inner resources when external stimulation is removed.

But today we learn a new way?

Why not? It's never too late to learn, though it does get harder with the passing years. We get more resistant to breaking our patterns.

But now we stop.

Here we are.

Change gear.

We sit still and notice. We notice the landscape around us and the inscape within us and become as a lake, settling after a storm. Occasional gusts of wind unsettle our water, but gradually calm comes. And just as still water reflects the sky, so the still mind reveals our true self.

Welcome home.

P.S. If you were a lake now, what sort of lake would you be?

36. Openness

Should we be open to everything?

Today we consider what it means to be open.

Good idea, because I get confused about this.

Openness is often spoken about in a positive way but what sort of a virtue is it?

Exactly. Is it healthy to be open to everything?

What gold, if any, lies at the end of this yellow brick road?

⁂

We're encouraged to bring a sense of openness to our solitude. But what does this mean?

I was hoping you were going to tell me.

I remember someone saying that an open mouth only has value if it closes on something solid.

So is the only purpose of openness to find something solid to close down around?

What do you think?

I don't know. But if it isn't – if instead we're to be open to everything without trying to distinguish dross from gold – then don't we become like a jelly fish in the ocean?

Jelly fish which absorb everything, yet in substance, are nothing very much?

Yes. In other words, is openess just a polite word for a parasitic state of indecision and weakness?

I take your point and in search of an answer we're going to make a rather gruesome historical detour.

Not too dark, I hope.

Maybe the darkness is important.

✳

You will have heard of The Inquisition.

Yes.

This was the organisation which in 14th and 15th century Europe, was granted power by the church to question people for deviancy from the true faith.

What were the rules for interrogation?

Well, this is the thing. In its infinite mercy – forgive the irony – the church commanded that no blood could be shed in the questioning but that pain was permissable.

This is loving your neightbour?

So while the church made itself feel better by ruling out the spilling of blood, it did allow the use of red hot pokers, the gouging out of eyes, the crushing of bodies by weights and the ripping of ligaments on the rack.

Why are you telling me this?

No doubt some inquisitors enjoyed the power and others found low-grade pleasure in causing pain. But most inquisitors were probably able to rationalise their behaviour.

How?

They would claim their actions were justified because they served a higher cause. After all, what could be more important than Christ's church on earth? The gouging, burning and crushing was Christ's work!

Unbelievable.

It is in a way. But before we get too judgmental we note that we do similar things. We may not do it with red hot pokers but like the Inquisition, we always find reasons for what we do. In a dispute or clash with someone else, we tend to imagine ourselves as the good guys and reckon our reactions to be entirely justified – which is exactly how the Inquisition worked.

I suppose so, but you started out with some questions about openness.

I did. And I believe we're now ready for some answers.

*

Some of the most famous words ever uttered in the English parliament were spoken in the 17th century by Oliver Cromwell to the MP's gathered there.

And the words were?

'I beseech you in the bowels of Christ, think it possible you may be mistaken.'

If taken seriously, that's a challenging thought.

It is openness to this possibility which above all else we take into solitude.

You're inviting us to be open to the possibility that we're wrong?

Yes.

Forgive me, but that's not a very appealing idea.

Ask only if it's helpful. As we reflect on the situations we've faced, it's helpful if we do not immediately ally ourselves and our cause with the truth.

What else can we do?

Instead, we listen for a while. Solitude is the willingness to penetate illusion at any price, to be open to the possibility of anything – even the possibility of being mistaken.

But some would say that a spiritual person is a certain person, a figure of certainty.

That would not be where I start. I recognise people of the spirit when I meet those prepared to be displeased with themselves; those who think it possible they may be mistaken.

And what's the opposite of people of the spirit?

People of the lie – people too frightened to contemplate even the smallest crack in their nice shiny shell.

*

But if I am content to be displeased with myself - isn't that the same as self-loathing?

Not at all.

Why not?

There is no health in self-loathing and that is not what I describe here. Rather, I describe someone who in solitude can listen on the wind.

And if the wind brings news of their own fallibility?

Then they can receive that news with grace and perhaps even plant it in soil where it might grow into a thing of beauty. That is a confident and hopeful inner state far from the netherworld of self-loathing, which we'll reflect on more in the next chapter.

You're talking about being able to receive things?

Indeed. 'Make your ego porous,' says Rainer Maria Rilke. 'Will is of little importance, complaining is nothing, fame is nothing. Openness, patience, receptivity, solitude is everything.'

In the sunshine of such openness, we see our defensive lies dissolve and watch beautiful attitudes grow.

Perhaps that gentle light can shine on you now.

37. Self-loathing or humility?

Can you endure anything but yourself?

In *The Devil's Dictionary,* Ambrose Bierce defines the word 'alone' as 'in bad company.'

Hah!

It's a joke with power because it flirts with the truth.

That's exactly what some people believe.

I suspect Ambrose Bierce himself believed it and it explains why solitude is such an unattractive proposition for people. If you think you're bad, you'll try and escape this uncomfortable thought rather than sit down alone with it.

You feel you can endure anything but yourself!

It's a theme taken up by J.Krishnamurti: 'You try being alone,' he writes, 'without any form of distraction and you will see how quickly you want to get away from yourself and forget what you are.'

So Ambrose Bierce has definitely struck a nerve.

But has he struck yours? Does self-loathing ring bad bells for you?

*

Let's step back a moment.

OK.

Solitude is the deliberate absence of others to encourage the fulness of ourselves.

That's a positive take on it.

And justified. There is rich significance in our lives and sometimes we must withdraw to recover a sense of it.

But are there rules about how we use our solitude?

There's the guidance of experience but no rules. It's important that we ourselves decide what we do with our solitude.

Why?

Because this is our fulness rather than the fulness of another. We are not someone else's story. We are our own story and we are a good story.

That all sounds a bit strange, a bit alien.

Well, it's good you notice that. But if it does sound alien to your ears, then you've been well taught in the art of self-loathing.

Taught? I never had self-loathing classes at school!

Most of our learning did not happen at school. But that doesn't mean the lessons didn't happen or that you're free from their impact now.

How do you mean?

Your psychological make-up is not a matter of chance but simple cause and effect. People do not hate themselves out of the blue; it's something they are taught, long before they make it to school.

How were they taught?

They did not feel valued at a young age; this was their perception. This experience when young is now forgotten by the mind, but internalised in the body. As adults, they still swim in the sea of their childhood feelings. So they may be 43 years old but emotionally they're nearer the age of four.

That's shocking. But how do you get out of the water – and get beyond the age of four?

Self-loathing is a hard lie to let go of. And we note that it's usually accompanied by cynicism which is another word for despair.

So cynicism is a symptom of self-loathing?

Yes and it's always good to notice the symptoms of an illness. The symptoms help diagnosis.

*

I used to think my friend was humble until I realised he just hated himself.

Self-loathing is often mistaken for humility. One response to self-loathing is a slightly depressed and withdrawn manner which can appear self-effacing and therefore humble. But humility and self-loathing are not related at all.

How do they differ?

Self-loathing is a depressed sickness; humility, a happy virtue. Self-loathing was put in us by others and is a borrowed feeling; whereas humility is our work and a sweet triumph of reality over delusion.

How do you mean?

Let's listen to a voice from the 14th century: 'In itself, humility is a true knowledge and awareness of oneself as one really is,' says *The Cloud of Unknowing*. 'It is undoubtedly true that if anyone could see and know themselves as they are, they would be truly humble.'

So how is humility happy?

Only the secure, only those who feel loved and safe in the world, can dare look at themselves warts and all.

Whereas the self-loathing cannot look at themselves at all?

No. Instead, they assume things about themselves and every assumption is borrowed and every assumption a lie.

*

My contradictions can get me down and make me feel ridiculous.

We've always carried contradictions within us and will continue to do so. But in allowing them rather than denying them, we transcend them.

Doesn't Thomas Merton say something about that?

He does. 'We are not meant to resolve all our contradictions,' he says, 'but to live with them and rise above them and see them in the light of exterior and objective values which make them trivial by comparison.'

Like wood smoke in a forest, we are to rise above our poor opinion of ourselves?

That is the call. In silence, we remove the old cloak of self-loathing and wrap ourselves in the warm folds of self-acceptance.

The old cloak was ridden with the lice of other people's behaviour. Our new clothes are fresh and smell of homecoming – a coming home to ourselves.

38. Solitary

Is it all right to be solitary sometimes?

Whatever we may imagine, we are all solitaries.

Really?

We alone live in our skin and we alone will die in it, hopefully having made some sense of it all and found some joy in it all.

Some of us do have friends, you know.

Of course, we're surrounded by others. A few we know quite well, some not so well and others hardly at all. But even in the crowd we remain solitaries, unable to speak our secrets, just as those around us are unable to speak theirs.

How so?

If we try to speak them, they change their meaning in another's ears; for their skin is not our skin and they hear in different ways.

You mean we are destined to be misunderstood?

Without getting all 'woe is me!' there is an element of that. Once we offer a personal truth to the world, we're aware it can be heard in a thousand different ways. As a priest, people would often thank me – and condemn me - for saying things I hadn't said!

They had heard different meanings in your words?

What people hear is only partially determined by what we say. As TS Eliot reminds us: 'All significant truths are private truths. As they become public, they cease to be truth; they become facts, or at best part of the public character; or at worst, catch words.'

Give an example.

When Jesus used the phrase 'born again' it had nothing of the meaning it is given now. When he spoke it, it was a phrase denoting adventure; now it has become a small and restrictive word in the public consciousness, a 'party' word used by a Christian sect, brutalised and in many mouths, a word of abuse.

It's true. There is something about our humanity that is impossible to communicate. Jesus could use the phrase, but he couldn't control the understanding of others or what it would become.

This truth makes a mature understanding of solitude all the more helpful.

Why?

It shows that solitude is not a sideshow to our lives, an optional extra for those who like that sort of thing. Rather, it's an experience at the heart of all aspects of our life.

For each of us is a solitary in a way.

And no matter how many roles you play in life, it's important you meet your solitary self who plays the most crucial role of all. Journey well with them and all else will be a good deal more manageable and merry.

*

So we're all solitaries – but we differ in what is possible for us and what is helpful for us. We don't all have to go to the desert to be hermits?

No. And we don't have to be starry-eyed about those who did go into the desert. We've talked warmly about the desert dwellers of the 4th century. But there were characters there who used the holy setting for their own purposes.

Didn't some leave their monasteries after a while and head off for a more solitary life in the mountain caves?

They did, but this is what I mean when I talk about people using a holy setting for their own purposes.

It sounds rather noble from where I'm sitting.

Maybe. But why we do things is much more important than what we do.

How do you mean?

Such apparently virtuous action did not always impress the insightful Mother Syncletica:

'There are many who live in the mountains,' she writes, 'yet behave as if they were in the towns and they are wasting their time. It is possible to be a solitary in one's mind while living in a crowd and it is possible for one who is a solitary to live in the crowd of his own thoughts.'

She's right about that.

So we note her warning but also find ourselves encouraged. We don't have to go to the big desert to be a solitary for 'it is possible to be a solitary in one's mind while living in a crowd.'

*

And as our isolation leads us into fresh life, we will give from what we receive.

You mean being a solitary isn't all about us?

The solitary is solitary for the world. Like a flowing river, we can only receive as we give, water replacing water.

The river must let go of water to receive water?

Giving creates space for receiving - as true for the solitary as for anyone else.

And the flow of the river within then flows out into the world?

As Lambros Kamperides says: 'The hermit has an obligation to offer to the world what he has received as enlightenment in his isolation.'

It's time to sit with the river that is your solitary self.

39. Busy

Why do I do the things I do?

'Kill your activities and still your faculties if you would realise the birth of God in you,' says Meister Eckhart.

But instead of killing our activities, we allow them to kill us.

Why?

＊

Imagine you're in a quiet room in the west country of England.

OK. What's happening?

Wendy is meeting her therapist.

That all sounds very nice.

Not at the moment. Wendy doesn't feel the therapist is being very helpful. He has raised the subject of Wendy's busy life. This has struck a raw nerve and now Wendy is fighting back:

'Isn't everyone busy?' she asks pointedly. 'Being busy is a good thing, surely?'

There's a pause, before the therapist replies:

'Being busy is what might be called a 'soft addiction' and is all the more dangerous for that.'

'How do you mean?' says Wendy.

'If it was a hard addiction, like drugs, people might take note and act. But with soft addictions - addictions that society deems entirely acceptable - no one will ever ring alarm bells on your behalf.'

'So who should ring the alarm bells?'

'The alarm bells can only be rung by you.'

'I'm fine. I'm not ringing any alarm bells.'

'And why would you ring them, Wendy, when the idea of stopping being busy fills you with such fear?'

*

We tend to be busy on various levels. This means we do not have time to contemplate who we are as people, let alone those we live and work with.

We have leisure time.

We do, but it's surprising how busy our leisure time can be. Busy people are busy whether at work or away from work. They take their busy life into their leisure, squeezing everything in. They're quite oblivious to how their behaviour distances themselves from themselves – even if they're only busy with TV.

But a holiday is a holiday!

Maybe. But consider how we use our holidays. If we go on holiday and read 14 novels by the pool or spend the week in determined and daring water sports or visit every ruin within a 50 mile radius – it is a rest of sorts.

Only 'of sorts'?

Well, we just note that it's all rather busy. Reading by the pool, we busy ourselves with other people's imaginary worlds; with the watersports, we busy ourselves with thrill and danger; and at the endless ruins, we busy ourselves with learning new things about previous civilisations.

I hadn't really thought of that as being busy.

What we make ourselves busy with varies, but the same thread runs throughout these adventures – the need to distract ourselves; the need to have something to do above contentment simply to be.

No sitting silent under the bodhi tree for us.

As Thich Nhat Hanh observes, 'We are not used to being with ourselves and we act as if we don't like ourselves and are trying to escape from ourselves.'

People do this at work and on holiday.

*

How do people justify this?

Those most determined to be busy always find a reason.

But how?

By a twisted alchemy, they turn the 'optional' into the 'necessary' and declare compulsive behavior to be virtuous behavior.

What do you mean?

Well, listen to this conversation:

'Why couldn't you sit quietly with your children?'

'I'd love to have done, believe me! But I had to go shopping for some bits and pieces and then just had a 101 other things to do!'

'You didn't have to do those things.'

'Someone has to do the work!'

'You chose to do them to fulfil your need of busyness. What are you frightened of?'

She wasn't being truthful about her motives?

As I say, what we do in life is not nearly as revealing as why we do it. And we explain away our actions to others and ourselves by making the optional seem necessary and our compulsion appear as virtue.

※

So are you against people doing things?

No.

Well, that's how it could appear.

This is not about doing less but about asking why we do the things we do.

That's a dangerous question to ask.

Perhaps. But isn't there enough fake virtue in the world without us adding to it with our compulsive busyness?

Fair point.

I know a man who drives a ten mile round trip to buy a pint of milk. His partner thinks it's because he loves her. The real reason is that she drives him up the wall and he likes to get out the house.

So our actions become a good deal purer, more joyful and creative as we allow ourselves to become aware of their origins?

Truthful action is action which does not have any reason other than itself; action which arises from the kiln of solitude with the dross of self-serving or disingenuous motives burned away.

And truthful action is infused with silence.

*

There are plenty of busy religious people, believe me!

You're right. We can bring our busyness into our search for God. But in doing so we push God ever further away.

How so?

Because in reality it's busyness we're worshipping. Busyness is our god so what room is there for the real thing?

The compulsively busy will stumble in their search for the holy?

'God will come to you so much sooner,' writes Angelus Silesius, 'if you will but stay completely still, instead of searching for him wildly until body and soul fall ill.'

So now, if we are able, we put our busyness in a boat and push it away downstream. We'll find it again but have no need of it for a while.

40. Labels

Is throwing away labels the first act of insight?

As adults, we must pretend to be grown-up to make our way in the world.

How do you mean?

Under the surface we're still at the bed-wetting stage, trying to cope with all our insecurities.

So what do we do?

Our survival method of choice tends to be labels. We stick them on ourselves, we stick them on others and others stick them on us.

That's a lot of labelling

It is and in our solitude today, we consider how helpful these labels are. Off the top of your head, can you think of five labels that either you give to yourself or that others give you?

*

We start by noting that ultimately labels are meaningless and a falsi-fication of the mystery that is our world.

Explain, sir!

Consider the label 'single mum'.

Well that's clear enough.

Is it?

It's certainly widely used.

But what does it mean? What does it tell us about the individual? It could, for instance, describe a woman happy to be without a husband, who feels content alone, with a well-paid job in a law firm and a mother close by for child care duties.

OK.

Or it could describe a desperately lonely woman on a housing estate where she is cut off from her family, with three children by three different fathers and still being physically abused by one of them.

Different, I grant you.

Or it could describe a woman who is divorced from her husband but who remains good friends with him and shares the upbringing of their children, including family holidays.

Different again.

So really, what does the label 'single mum' tell us?

I take your point.

And it's the same with religious labels. There are so many types of Christians, Buddhists, Muslims and Hindus that they all have labels within labels! To label someone 'Christian' reveals little more than the label 'single mum'.

But we go on using them.

And not just using them, but relying on them, shaping our lives by them.

*

But we like our labels.

We do, yes. Like a castle, they can be reassuring walls to hide behind. And on occasion we can use them to demonise others in order to feel good about ourselves. It makes me feel wise if I can label you an 'idiot'.

You wouldn't be the first.

But in a mystery world, labels brutalise the truth and in a changing world, they stagnate the truth.

I beg your pardon?

OK, we'll pause a moment and reflect on Plato.

Who I've heard of, but don't know much about.

Check the brief biography at the back, but it was Plato who described the visible world as a place where nothing lasts and nothing stays the same.

Interesting.

As he liked to put it, everything in this world is always becoming something else. This formulation became shortened to 'everything is becoming, nothing is.'

I see where this is going. Labels, even if they catch a moment, are quickly out of date?

They are, yes. In such a world, labels are temporary affairs, for tomorrow the world will have changed and so will we. We are people who are becoming but a label wants us fixed.

I can see what you mean about their stagnating effect.

Buddha told a story about this long before Plato lived. He said that just because a life-raft had got a man to the shore, he did not then need to carry the life-raft on his shoulders as he travelled across land.

The life-raft had done its work and he should let go of it?

Buddha felt people clung on to ideas long after they had ceased to be useful. The ideas may have had their moment; but the moment has passed.

✳

We go to a court room scene.

Ooh, I like court room scenes.

The judge has just asked the defendant's age.
'I'm 18, sir,' he says.
'Really?'
'I'm 18, sir.'
'But how can I believe you?' says the judge. 'You've been saying you're 18 for the last ten years!'
'I certainly have, sir,' says the defendant with pride. 'I'm not one of those people who says one thing one year and quite another thing the next!'

Nice one.

There's a season for everything. We needn't worry about saying something different to what we said last year. Seasons change and we change because that is the nature of things. Last year the baby drank milk. This year the child eats solids.

And solitude can help in all this?

Solitude is a good place to loosen ourselves from the netherworld of labels. Just as we leave people behind in solitude, let us also leave labels behind, for we have no need of them here.

Which might be a big relief.

Indeed. And as we look back on our life, we notice how seasons come and go. It's often only in solitude that we notice their passing and feel able to peel off a label that has been there too long – whether it's one we have given to ourselves or one others have stuck on us.

The trouble is, there's no one to tell us when our labels die.

No, they just grow cold and sometimes we notice.

41. Where is God?

How do you experience God these days?

I don't believe in God.

That's OK, but we're still doing the chapter. Apart from anything else, I don't know what the 'God' label means to you, so I'm not sure what you're rejecting.

Maybe I'm not either.

Stay or go as you feel comfortable; but we'll be reflecting on the human search for God.

OK.

*

There's a famous scene in the Hebrew Scriptures. Elisha is in the desert where there is a rock-shattering wind, but God is not in the wind. This is followed by a loud earthquake but God is not in the earthquake. There is then an outbreak of fire, but God is not in the fire.

After the fire, comes a still small voice, barely audible but clear as light. God is finally speaking.

It was an important story at the time. The idea that God was in the quiet and still rather than the violent and noisy was a real break with tradition. And it's still breaking with tradition today. Stillness does not feature much in religious gatherings.

✳

Of course, in the Hebrew scriptures everything was attributed to God. Did it thunder? Then God was angry. Did the Israelites lose a battle? Then God was not with them. Did a rival king die of a heart attack? Celebrate! It was God at work!

These days, however, it's different: nothing is God. If you recover from illness, it's the pills. If you feel happy, it's the chemicals in your brain. If the flowers are beautiful, it's a chance occurrence in a random universe.

So where is God these days? And is that a question you can relate to?

✳

Atheists say there is no God and agnostics say we cannot be sure. But what do the major religions say? Buddhists say 'Now' is God while Judaism, Christianity and Islam turn it round and say God is now.

There is difference in them. They explore different paths and take different routes up the mountain of faith. They use different guides and different maps. But there is something primal in their agreement: that God can only be found now, or alternatively, that now is the divine moment.

✳

I just find religion a bit hysterical.

Oh, you're here?

I thought I'd hang around. But I don't like it when religion stirs people up in ridiculous frenzies.

I take your point but you don't find frenzy in the teaching of Buddha or Jesus. In Jesus' teaching, God does not have to be invoked or begged for. His famous 'Our father' prayer is short and simple, quite without hysteria. It assumes God is not distant but close. Whatever you're doing, and wherever your heart might be, God is now. It's simple, not hysterical.

But everyone loves their own version of God.

That's a pretty normal response to life. Everyone likes their own version of everything.

How do you mean?

Everyone likes their own book collection, their own music collection, their own DVD collection and so on. So it's not surprising they bring their preferences to God.

Which is a problem.

It is what it is. But God is skilled at getting out of the straigth jackets he gets put in. He's a fast God who tends to keep moving. 'Burn every address for God,' as Hafiz says because he has no address.

He does in some places. I've just been reading a book about Gandhi and I think of the battles he had as he tried to bring a peaceful end to British rule in India.

It's true. Gandhi lived amid the fires of conflicting religious certainties. God and politics mixed freely and explosively in India in the 1930's and 1940's with all sides claiming absolute truth and God for themselves.

And Gandhi's view?

For Gandhi, truth was God but only God knew the absolute truth.

He recommended caution?

'Truth is God but God alone knows the absolute truth,' he said. 'We can only pursue relative truth.' But he also believed that if our search is pure and devoid of self-interest, then we'll come to no harm.

But a search that is pure and devoid of self-interest is hard. No, I'd go further and declare it impossible – we should give up on God.

＊

Alongside the question 'Where is God?' is another question: 'Where are you?' Because you're quite as much part of this story as any god.

Convince me.

We may think we know enough about God either to deny his existence or to affirm his existence. We may have read books about God, heard stories, analyzed the evidence and drawn our own conclusions. But until we've left our analyzing minds behind and arrived in the present, we cannot meet God - the idea is ridiculous.

Why so? Analysis is important.

God cannot be thought.

Why not?

God lives in the now where the mind is unable to go. The human brain is formed by past experiences and so it's either looking back in assessment or projecting forward in planning. It has no capacity for present encounter and fears it.

This is why *The Cloud of Unknowing* says God can be met through love but never via thought. 'Of God himself,' he says, 'no man may think. By love he may be grasped and held, by thought never.'

It was a shock to some of his bookish contemporaries whose entire understanding of God was stored in their expert thoughts.

＊

Once people believe they know where God is they tend to clothe him in a distinctive way and the various traditions use various wardrobes. Ultimately, however, God remains naked, unclothed by our mental assumptions and beyond our grand declarations.

That's a convenient assertion.

Convenient for who?

It makes God untouchable.

It makes God unknowable.

*

We started today with God discovered in a still small voice. We close with God discovered in silence: 'There's nothing so much like God in all the universe as silence,' says Meister Eckhart.

And solitude is the path to silence?

42. Community

Who are the dangerous people in your community?

'Community and solitude are like chalk and cheese, oil and water. They don't mix! You have to choose between them.'

That's what some people say and I can see their point.

But Dietrich Bonhoeffer thought differently. He discerned a close link between the two: 'Let him who cannot be alone beware of community. He will only do harm to himself and the community.'

Does this ring any bells?

We all live in communities, whether it's our school, office, factory, street, yoga class, football team, staircase, book club, monastery or home.

And what has solitude got to do with those?

In solitude, we create and nurture the person we take into our community.

I see.

And in particular, we nurture inside ourselves a circle approach rather than a square approach.

Hang on, this is a new idea. What are you talking about?

I'm contrasting a square spirituality with a circle spirituality. Simply put, if our spirituality is square, we face only four particular directions; if our spirituality is a circle, we face every direction.

And?

The square approach is selective and honours a few; the circle approach is inclusive and honours all.

So the question is: who do you honour in the communities of which you are part?

*

The circle spirituality is a picture of openness.

It is, yes, and we'll handle such openness in different ways.

It can't be the same for the introvert as it is for the extrovert.

No. For the introvert, the circle calling will appear exhausting and provide a particular challenge.

How will they handle it?

The healthy introvert will work to nurture a generous and outgoing spirit within themselves even if they cannot always manage the engaging chattiness of the extrovert. A generous and open inner spirit communicates in its own ways.

And for the extrovert, it's all easy?

Extroverts have their own issues in communities. They'll be the ones who tend to get noticed, but if life in the community is being used to avoid an experience of solitude, then there's danger. If we use our communities to seek attention rather than silence, then we are using others for our own unhealthy purposes.

And as Bonhoeffer says, we become both a danger to ourselves and them.

✳

So how do we go about this circle calling?

We'll each find our own way for spirituality is not 'one size fits all.'

Thank goodness.

Spirituality exists to serve us; we do not exist to serve spirituality. But whether introvert, extrovert or a bit of both, the circle approach is the goal of all. It's endlessly attractive and welcoming to those around, however expressed.

✳

It's the circle spirituality we look after in solitude.

Does it need looking after?

I think so. Life can beat us senseless and leave our circle looking a lot like a square; or indeed, something so broken that it's no discernible shape at all.

It was the Japaneses hermit Ryoken who said: 'It is not that I dislike people; it is just that I am so tired of them.'

Here, here!

We can all identify with his sentiments; and sometimes it's hard for our weariness not to mutate into dislike. We lose the energy to love and like a rotting lily, move from beauty to decay.

Indeed, sometimes we're looking in no other direction than that of fear, fury, worry or spite.

We're staying real. That's a relief.

As ever, we notice what is happening inside us. We note that life has left us less than we are, less than we might be and strangers to ourselves. We duly take ourselves away from community, away from others to the healing sounds of silence.

*

I close with a story.

Happy or sad?

Sad in a way, though it's not over so who knows?

What's it about?

I was recently at a gathering of friends.

Nice.

It was, yes. But although I sat next to one of them, we didn't meet.

How was that?

She wasn't there.

What do you mean, 'She wasn't there'?!

'Somehow she just isn't there when I talk with her,' said another friend and I know what they mean.

Over the years, her 'front' has become her only reality. I suspect she's a rather frightened person and has cut herself off from any relationship with her inner self. Instead, she opts for a half-smiling persona which she takes like fragile glass out into the world.

Yes, I think I can identify with that experience.

This has consequences. 'When one is a stranger to oneself then one is estranged from others too,' writes Anne Morrow Lindbergh. 'If one is out of touch with oneself then one cannot touch others. Only when one is connected to one's own core is one connected to others...and for me, the core, the inner spring can best be found through silence.'

So a sad story.

Well, maybe. But no story is ever over and perhaps in time my friend and I will meet again.

It's strange, but from the way you talk, in solitude we come home to community.

43. Self-mastery

Am I alienated from my deepest needs?

The routine of solitude is part of a stilling of life and a simplifying of life. It's also the cradle of self-mastery.

I hope you're going to explain what you mean.

*

There was a man called Larry who had a fish pond. And he wished to fill it with gorgeous fish.

Is this one of your stories?

It is, yes. So Larry went to the gorgeous fish seller and bought three of her finest. Proudly he took the fish home and put them in his pond. But when he visited the pond the following morning, he made a terrible discovery: the gorgeous fish were dead.

Furious, Larry went back to the gorgeous fish seller and complained. She said they had been her best fish, but gave him three more anyway. Excitedly he took them home, sure now that everything would be all right.

But when he visited the pond the following morning, another terrible discovery awaited him: it had happened again - the gorgeous fish had all died!

Incensed, he returned to the gorgeous fish seller, whose reputation was second to none.

'Your second batch of gorgeous fish was as bad as your first!' declared Larry. 'They died as well! I demand a refund! I demand more fish! I demand - '

At this point the gorgeous fish seller interrupted his indignation. 'Have you ever thought of changing the water?' she asked.

*

Is this story about self-mastery?

In a way.

How so?

We love to acquire fresh insights but we do not wish to change ourselves. This is why our exciting new insights do not excite us for very long; they must live – and die – in our unchanged selves.

*

Self-mastery is the art of changing our water and it begins in solitude. It's here we develop the discipline to return ourselves to ourselves.

Return ourselves to ourselves? That just sounds ridiculous.

That's for you to decide. But Anthony Storr thinks it less ridiculous than you do. His own experience as a psychiatrist led him to believe that people could end up a long way from themselves.

Well, I'm open to other views. What does he say?

'Human beings,' he writes 'easily become alienated from their own deepest needs and feelings. Learning, thinking, innovation and maintaining contact with one's own inner world are all facilitated by solitude.'

He's saying a lot there. So when exactly do we lose ourselves?

We're always losing ourselves. It's a daily occurrence. It happens when our desires become distorted by the ego; when our mind runs in different directions and when our attention becomes a weak and distracted thing.

So self-mastery is concerned with our desires, our minds and our attention?

There are laws in the universe and self-mastery is returning our selves to happy harmony with those laws.

Give an example.

If, for instance, our desires have wandered from love, then our desire has lost its way. If our mind has wandered from stillness, then our mind has lost its way. If our attention to the present has become sporadic, then our attention has lost its way.

In each instance, we work against the laws of the universe and exchange sanity for insanity.

*

It seems you're advocating a new intelligence in us?

I think you're right. In the strength and calm of solitude we approach life with a new intelligence, a spiritual intelligence. We become less obsessed by new fish, new ideas. We have used these as a distraction for too long, and we don't need any more. As one frustrated person said to me: 'I've read all the books, been on all the courses and I'm still exactly the same!'

So what do you suggest?

Instead of seeking endless new fish, we look more closely at the water we throw our fish into; and change in our water occurs as we notice the cause of the pollution.

Our desires, our minds, our attention?

Yes. In solitude we lead our desires back to love, our mind back to stillness and our attention back to the present. In so doing, we find ourselves in balance and harmony with the universe once again.

That could interrupt a few of our plans.

Then so be it. Abandon them; they were probably only a distraction anyway.

*

I was once sent a card.

So you do have a friend?

On the front of the card, in bold print, were the words: 'You are the answer to my prayers!' And then on the inside it read: 'You're not what I asked for – but you appear to be the answer.'

Those in the foothills of self-mastery will be able to laugh.

44. Recovering our story

Isn't it time you had feelings of your own?

What follows is the outline of a conversation I've had many times with different people. The details may vary on each occasion, but the thrust of the exchange is the same.

So we can listen in?

Be my guest.

'Robert, your life seems dominated by internal voices,' I say.
'I don't hear any voices,' says Robert. 'What do you mean?'
'As you tell me about your life, I hear strong negative feelings, feelings full of fear - and those feelings appear to be running your life.'
'I have strong feelings, sure.'
'And each of those feelings is like a voice inside you.'
'Oh, I see. Well, maybe.'
'That's how they work. They tell you what mood to adopt and you obey, even though it makes you unhappy.'
'It's not that simple to change, Simon.'
'I think it is simple. But also hard.'
'How do you mean?'
'It's simple in that you know there are feelings inside you which make you unhappy.'
'Yes. So?'
'So clearly you didn't put them there.'
'Why do you say that?'

'You wouldn't put feelings inside yourself which make you unhappy. Someone else put them there.'

'Someone else put my feelings inside me?'

'Yes.'

'How?'

'You've internalised other people's voices and attitudes. You've internalized voices you heard around you when you were small and attitudes you experienced. Now you imagine they are who you are.'

'But they are who I am!'

'No, as I say, they are external voices and attitudes which you have internalised; borrowed ideas from your past which you have never really questioned. But they're not yours.'

'Which feelings do you mean?'

'Well, take one example: whatever happens in your life, Robert, you have a problem with it. You can never celebrate it. There's a deep strain of negativity inside you.'

'It's true my mother was very negative, very fearful. She never believed anything would work out – '

' – and she's still telling you that, despite being dead 13 years. Each time you heard that voice as a boy, it became a little more internalized, until over time, you forgot the original voice and just had the feeling.'

'I feel uncomfortable here. I don't want to be disloyal to my parents.'

'That's a common response but this is not about disloyalty - it's about honesty. We encourage people to be honest in every other area of their lives. Why should we suddenly change the rules with parents?'

'Well, it's not right, is it?'

'Really? You must decide that for yourself. Many do close down, it's true. They decide to leave their personal story well alone. They choose unhappiness over honesty and that choice is open to you.'

'Well, when you put it like that –'

'How else can I put it? The opposite of honesty is denial which is a bleak place both for yourself and those who have to live with you.'

'But it's like I'm blaming my parents.'

'It isn't about blame, Robert, though it may feel like that at first. It's about you and your life now. Recovering your story is about you finally taking responsibility for your self – which any healthy parent, any loving parent would wish for you.'

'It's just the fear, really. I'm fearful of stirring that particular water. It feels like the last battle.'

'You must decide what you want. But maybe it feels like the last battle because after that you will be free.'
'I'm not sure what it is to be free.'
'Don't you at least think it's time you had your own feelings about life?'

*

In solitude, we notice some of the feelings that have arisen in us recently.

I know someone who does this at the end of each day.

That's helpful because each feeling is a voice or attitude from the past, internalised. Perhaps we can still hear the voice and remember how we felt at the time; or perhaps it was too frightening or disturbing and we buried it, leaving us with a feeling we can't now explain.

But now we note the borrowed feeling and consider if it's a loan we wish to continue?

That's right. And as our breathing settles, things borrowed tend to dissolve in the sound of silence.

45. Distraction

How distracted am I?

We start today with some striking words from the desert father, Father Anthony:

'Who wishes to dwell in the solitude of the desert is delivered from three conflicts: hearing, speech and sight.'

So what do you think?

I don't know what he's talking about.

That's one response and it can appear an odd message, I grant you. He's saying that hearing, speech and sight must be considered as conflicts, as distractions.

That's my point. They're not distractions - they're the stuff of life!

So who here is mad? Does Anthony make any sense at all? And is distraction an illness or a bit of harmless fun?

✳

I'm going to talk about hermits again.

But no one reading this is a hermit.

That's quite possible. But this book is a bridge from activity to silence and whatever we think of their calling – whether we're romantic or cynical about it - the hermit has more experience of this path than we do.

That may be true.

So they have insight into the process. We may not wish to leave the world as the hermit has done; but neither do we wish to be quite so defined by the world as we presently are.

*

Aren't hermits into poverty, fasting and chastity?

Those are big themes, yes. There is something stripped down about the hermit's life.

How do these practices help?

They simplify and they focus. They remove the hermit from the world's means of definition.

How so?

A commitment to poverty relieves them from scanning the stocks and shares and interest rates. They are not defined by their income.

True.

While fasting focuses the attention.

And makes you hungry.

Fasting may involve food but more important is the fast from unhelpful attitudes.

And chastity?

Chastity frees them from what the desert fathers called 'sensuousness'.

Sensuousness?

They used the word in a different way from us. Sensuousness had a bigger meaning, describing not just sexual attraction but any contact with a human and the emotional baggage they carry. Simply put, the hermit was not to busy themselves with other people's lives - a classic way of avoiding their own.

I suppose people were keen to seek the counsel of hermits.

Oh yes and some were eager to give it. Many anecdotes from the desert tell of abbots protecting hermits from well-meaning visitors – or from themselves. For the true solitary, familiarity with anyone is a distraction, 'a strong burning wind' across the sweet orchards of his or her contemplation.

✳

They took withdrawal seriously.

They were certainly aware of human psychology. These people did not have twitter or mobile phones but they recognized the dangers of social networking in the desert; noticed how we love to let people draw us in.

How do you mean?

We are nosey or controlling about other people's lives and dress it up as concern.

Ah, yes!

Or we gossip about others and call it sharing. We do these things to give honour to the way we use other people to distract our selves from our selves.

And in solitude?

In solitude we take leave of these people and die to our obsession with them and with all created things. As Meister Eckhart said, 'Who ever

possesses the world least, actually possesses it the most. No one owns the world as much as they who have given the whole world up.'
This is good psychology in whatever century it appears.

＊

How do we know when we are not distracted?

We are not distracted when we are content to do the one thing, whatever it is. We do one thing at a time and contemplate one thing at a time. I can imagine watching one TV show in solitude, but not two. One programme could become a meditation; two programmes pull you in different directions and are therefore a distraction which literally means 'a pulling apart'.

Similarly, I could imagine you reading one chapter of this book in a session but not two. One chapter might focus your attention on something; two chapters would over-stimulate and scatter you inside.

＊

But no hearing, no speech, no sight?

Yes. According to Father Anthony, the desert hermits were to be free of 'conflicts' such as these.

And here, across the centuries, is a challenging glimpse of the journey into ever-deepening silence. In the search for the still place, in search of our selves, we do not merely leave people behind; we also leave behind our restless senses.

＊

'He who delights in solitude is either a wild beast or a god,' says Francis Bacon.

Meaning?

They're a beast because they're temperamentally incapable of human contact or a god, because their truest self lies beyond human contact.

As I say, most of us are not hermits. Or maybe we are amateur hermits and as novices in the practice of solitude we can learn from the experts. We may think them insane but their focused insanity is perhaps less mad than our distracted sanity.

For a moment, we push back the foliage of distraction and set our compass towards silence beyond.

46. Peace

Is peace a familiar friend to you?

I'll start with a quotation again today.

Have you run out of your own ideas?

Thankfully, yes and it's a huge relief. I'm aware I can't improve on the wisdom already out there. All I can do is move them from the Exhibits Shelf and put them to work.

Fair enough. So what's the quote?

'Out of the crooked timber of humanity a straight thing can never be made,' says Immanuel Kant.

Well, there's a cheerful start! If I was reading this, I'd probably stop reading now and kill myself.

Slightly dramatic.

Possibly.

And of course they are cheerful words.

How on earth are they cheerful?

They're cheerful for being accurate. There's nothing more cheerful than accuracy because then you know where you stand.

True. Inaccurate directions are a nightmare.

And they're helpful words when considering peace, which we are today.

Why?

In our search for peace, we need a peace that accommodates our reality.

Meaning?

You said yourself you wanted to stay real.

I did.

So we need a peace that accommodates our crookedness rather than denies it. We need a peace able to grow in the soil of our imperfection. Is peace a familiar friend to you?

*

Does solitude bring peace?

Solitude may bring peace but the two words are far from interchangeable. Sometimes I lead retreats. They tend to be fairly silent events, but experience shows that for many people, they are anything but peaceful.

Why so?

Things that are repressed in the noise come to the surface in silence. So only the brave go on retreat.

And only the brave embark on solitude?

Yes. Solitude is a path to a beyond place, a place on the other side where our lives – and the lives of the world – can be held and contemplated.

Like trekking in Nepal, it's a higher plane but also a more rigorous one where people are found out.

How do you mean?

Do not imagine silence is easy or easily mastered. I think of Silvester who left his monastery to live as a hermit. He had felt himself called to higher things.

What could possibly go wrong?

But after a few weeks as a hermit, his high hopes began to fade. He found his solitude too demanding, too troubling and so he returned to his brothers in the monastery. But he couldn't find peace there either and so he visited the abbot Theodore of Pherme to talk with him about it.

'If you are not at peace when alone or with others, Silvester, why have you become a monk?'

Silvester could not answer so Theodore answered for him.

'Did you not become a monk to suffer trials?'

Silvester wasn't sure.

'Tell me,' said Theodore, 'how many years have you worn the habit?'
'Eight years.'
'Eight years? I have worn the habit 70 years,' he replied, 'and on no day have I found peace. Do you expect to obtain peace in eight years?'

*

The anecdote concludes by saying that Silvester went away encouraged.

That isn't my reaction.

I can understand that. Certainly we'll appreciate Theodore's honesty and lack of glib talk about peace, which sometimes spills too easily from people's lips. Speaking about peace is not the same as knowing peace.

That's true.

But as you imply, a big question presents itself: is it unreasonable to expect a few days of contentment among the abbot's 70 years of service?

You think that perhaps the story tells us more about Theodore than about Silvester the failed hermit?

*

Peace is not a commodity that you either possess or do not possess.

So it's not like owning a car?

No. Either you own a car or you don't own a car. But peace is more elusive. It's a quality we possess in differing degrees as the day does by. Like the tide on a beach, it ebbs and flows and we notice its progress and withdrawal along the shoreline of our soul. It can be quickly snatched – and quickly granted.

Where is the tide at present for you?

*

Equally, we acknowledge different sorts of peace.

How do you mean?

Sometimes we're overwhelmed by an emotional experience of utter well-being.

That's true.

On another occasion, it might simply be that we're facing a difficult situation as best we can, with good intentions and as much strength as we can muster. There is peace here too, though it may not feel especially good. It's peace carved from the rock rather than peace poured over us like annointing oil.

That's a good distinction.

Peace is a fragile state; it can be smashed in a moment and found in a moment. A simple word from someone can make a great difference to our inner terrain, either positively or negatively. And it's not always black and white. We can feel two things at once.

An example?

A relief worker in a famine-hit village will experience both peace and no-peace: peace that she is there, doing what is possible; no-peace at the starvation and suffering around her.

*

In solitude, we notice the coming and going of peace, this ebb and flow. We learn much about ourselves as we note what brings peace and what brings non-peace.

And if our peace is dependent on a nice meal or a full diary or the applause of friends?

Then perhaps we need to question the peace we've invented for ourselves. That sounds more like greed than peace.

And I suppose we begin to sense the blockages in us.

True. Why, for instance, had Abbot Theodore found no peace for 70 years? He was a follower of Jesus who said 'My peace I give you.' So clearly something was going wrong; something was working in him against peace.

His psychology needed some attention?

*

'Ministers of good things are like torches,' says Richard Hooker, 'a light to others; a waste and destruction to themselves.'

That's a bit savage.

He was speaking of people who spoke eloquently of peace to others but knew none for themselves.

Which is probably more common than we know.

Today, though, we think only of ourselves.

Good!

And today you are a minister of good things, so look after yourself. Burn bright but don't burn out.

And peace?

Seek truth on the path of solitude and peace will join you on the journey.

47. Power

What's my experience of power?

We walked inside the old castle. It was an awesome building with huge walls, thick beyond imagining. Here were tall turrets, slit windows, inner walls and outer walls. It was a massive presence of stone which spoke of power.

In the 13th century people built fortresses to tell everyone just how powerful they were.

They still do. Look at big business. It likes to house itself in sky scraper buildings.

True, though maybe a big bank account is now more important than big walls.

And the only armies needed are armies of accountants ensuring the best possible returns for investments.

So we're reflecting on power today.

OK.

*

There are different forms of power, of course and I'm now thinking of how people use status.

Don't get me started!

For many, the use and abuse of power is most often experienced at work. 'This is how things work here,' said one boss whose behaviour had been challenged. 'Accept it or leave.'

Others suffer from the status in the family hierarchy.

That's true. Parents have enormous power in the early years and children have none.

And then there's religion.

Yes, religion exercises power by creating beliefs and codes of conduct.

These are then protected by priesthoods and communities who require followers to toe the line and who use various methods to ensure they do.

Agreed. No organisation down the years has used the power of fear, guilt or hysteria as effectively as religion.

But it's not just organisations who misuse power, is it? Individuals play their own low-grade power games.

Correct. Humans are remarkable if damaged survivors and have learned their own ways of attack and defence, which do not need tall turrets or thick castle walls. One person might use the threat of their rage to keep the family cowering; others might use clever words or a negative spirit to keep people down.

And what about emotional manipulation? I've seen it. People playing the victim to achieve their ends or giving gifts with strings attached.

Power has so many guises. I know those who bring a controlling spirit to situations. Unable to control their inner world, they seek to control their outer world, commanding this and that, which is very unpleasant for everybody.

All in all, it's not a happy list, is it?

No. So how has power been for you? How do you use it? And how has it been used on you?

✽

It's good to be aware of our story.

How do you mean?

It's important to understand how people in our past have used their power over us. How we continue to let people to use their power over us will probably echo these experiences.

We get into patterns as children that it's hard to step out of, even as adults?

Certainly. How many women step into an abusive relationship with a partner who mirrors the behaviour of their father? It's what they know and are familiar with.

Yes, it's difficult to understand that.

But we all do it. In our relational choices we often prefer familiar death to unfamiliar life. We choose people who are what we know rather than people who will draw new and good things from us.

✽

But also significant here is how we use our power over others; the methods we use to attack others or defend our territory.

Most people think of themselves as the victims. They don't imagine they ever abuse their power. 'Me? Abusing power? Never!'

So in solitude we allow honesty and awareness to fall like the morning dew. We begin to remove the manacles we've allowed others to put on us and undo the manacles we've put on others.

218

If we have allowed the power of others to oppress us, then we allow that oppression to dissolve in the moment. Perhaps we imagine the manacles being undone.

That's hard.

It's both gradual and instant. We breathe in strength and breathe out the power these people held.

Breathe in strength?

We need to allow fresh winds into our psyche that disturb our inner scenery; fresh winds every day. The power we fear is a phoney power. Graveyards are full of people who once imagined they had power. They have no power now and in truth had only the pretence of power in their lives.

✻

'In solitude,' writes Laurence Sterne, 'the mind gains strength and learns to lean upon itself.'

'The mind gains strength and learns to lean upon itself?' I like that.

And as we gain strength, the strength of others has less power to invade or demand or frighten. We stop giving them power.

But we don't give it to them – they exert it!

No, we give it to them. People do not have power over us; we give it to them as a gift and this is never a good gift to give.

So today we take back the gift and reflect on the one power we do have.

What's that?

The power to live in the moment with awareness and acceptance. That is a truer authority than a castle wall, a sky scraper or the threat of a tantrum.

48. Enemies

Do I have enemies?

There is rarely a news bulletin that does not include an exploding bomb which kills people and threatens the fragile peace in that land.

I saw one reported yesterday.

Once again, two sides are polarised in their opposition and emotions run high. A bridge of peace that might have taken years to build is reduced to rubble in seconds.

So we're thinking about world peace?

No, we're thinking about ourselves, the only people we can change. We too know the exploding bomb of hatred and dislike in ourselves.

A tad dramatic.

It's not helpful for you to distance your self from strong feelings.

Me?

You well know the power of someone's behaviour to create powerful reactions in you and leave your peace shattered.

OK.

And you too feel the force of polarisation as you pull away from them in disgust or fury saying: 'How can they have done that?'

All right, all right. So can solitude help us as we face our enemies?

*

Having enemies is not unusual.

On reflection, I'm not sure I'd call them enemies.

What would you call them?

Well, 'people I struggle with' perhaps?

Sometimes we don't call them enemies because it doesn't sound nice. But if we were honest about our feelings, that's probably what they would be.

You mean we find it hard to be honest about our hostility?

You and many others. Sometimes people recount something done to them and I say: 'That must have made you very angry.'

And they can't admit it?

'Oh I wasn't angry,' they reply demurely, 'just disappointed.' Or, 'No, not angry – just sad; sad that they behave like that.'

We have many ways to dress up our aggressive feelings towards someone but at any given moment most of us have an enemy of some sort.

Even holy people?

Especially the holy! The best-selling spiritual writer Henri Nouwen writes candidly about his feelings as he lay in a hospital bed:

'In my mind's eye, I saw the men and women who aroused within me feelings of anger, jealousy and even hatred. They had a strange power over me. They might never think of me but every time I thought of them,

I lost some of my inner peace and joy. Their criticism, rejection or expression of personal dislike still affected my feelings about myself.'

I like his honesty.

Yes, sometimes the honesty of others helps us into a clearer understanding of ourselves.

*

So where does solitude come into the equation?

We must be aware of how we use our solitude. Some people sit alone in brooding silence and allow resentments to fester, which just makes things worse.

True. So what should we do with our enemies in solitude?

We risk something different: we're invited to imagine ourselves in generous relationship with them. We do not have to like what they do but we allow what they do because, quite simply, we do the same.

Do we?

We may not do what they do in the same way but in different ways we're alike. Are they being mean to us? Quite possibly, but we have been mean to others. Are they being cold towards us? Yes. But others have felt our coldness. Are they misusing their power? Probably. But have we never misused our power?

It's not comfortable but I can see shafts of truth's light there.

We do not have to like what they do; we may even challenge what they do. But we remember always that they are people and not enemies and people like us.

And that's a sense cultivated in the self-understanding of solitude?

*

Wise words are all fine and dandy but when it comes to hostility, well - we're talking about a strong emotion here!

I don't minimise the difficulties or the forces at work. Hostility is one of the brain's most primal survival tools. It appears early in human life and it's a force we struggle to control. We'll always have set backs in peace building whether in the world or in ourselves. The forces against peace and reconciliation are huge, within us and beyond us, and there will be body blows along the way.

That's my experience.

So we note also that our friends may not help.

Really?

As Abraham Lincoln observes, 'A friend is someone who has the same enemies as you'.

Guilty as charged!

This means that they may actually encourage us to demonise others.

And is that so bad?

Colluding with the negativity of another is a dull affair and never helpful. It's not the role of a friend to encourage or confirm us in our dislikes; a friend may allow us our dislikes but not encourage us to take them seriously.

*

'Never underestimate the power of a handshake,' says Archbishop Desmond Tutu for it's a glimpse of a new order.

In solitude we keep our enemies as people remarkably like us; and look them in the eye as we shake their hand.

49. Useless

Is being useless the worst thing in the world?

'There's a lot of it about,' said the woman at the bus stop and I nodded sagely.

What was happening?

It was a time when everyone seemed to be ill. Offices were half-empty with people either off sick or avoiding those who were.

And you?

I was ill at the time, yes. Struggling on but paying the price.

And egged on by self-important feelings of indispensability?

Maybe. My particular dose was a respiratory infection though I didn't know it at the time. For three weeks, I had been coughing like a Russian writer, but without their book sales and it all seemed slightly unfair.

Illness always seems unfair.

I was delivering on my various writing commitments, but a temperature arrived with dull precision every afternoon and evening and then I was fit for nothing and no one.

Some people rather enjoy being ill.

But not all. Those whose self-worth is found in what they do find it hard. If they're unable to do, they can feel threatened when weakness strikes. They're not content just to be.

*

So what happened to you in the end?

Finding a doctor was not easy. My own doctor didn't have a space for two weeks, and debating the matter on the phone didn't help. As ever, we must fight for these things when feeling at our weakest.

I'm trying to rustle up some sympathy.

Finally, in a small corner of a busy A&E department, I discovered an out-of-hours doctor service and the prescribed antibiotics did the rest: in a few days, my health was restored.

The power of science!

But not before at least one illusion had been shattered: the medic who saw me explained that all cough mixtures – which I had been drinking slavishly - were a complete waste of time and money.

What should you have been drinking?

'Water', he said. 'There's nothing better than water.'

Sometimes help is closer to hand than we think.

And cheaper.

*

So why are you telling me all this?

The fact is, I had some good times when ill.

It doesn't sound like it.

It's all about how you tell the story. On one level, of course, it's a nuisance. I had to keep ringing people to cancel engagements, while wondering if perhaps I was fit enough to attend. And then there was my inability to plan or promise anything, as a day of sickness became a week and then one week became two: 'How long, O Lord? I'm never ill! How can this be happening to me?'

So what was good about it?

Shining like a beacon in the darkness was a wonderful sense of uselessness.

Uselessness?

It was something I'd never expected to cherish. As I collapsed day after day, I felt like a passenger in the world, unable to contribute to the voyage and with no desire to do so. Nothing I had previously set my heart on had any meaning and it was all very liberating. I was useless but happy.

Strange.

*

I remember long ago being haunted by *The Stature of Waiting* by W H Vanstone. In this book, he compares the active and challenging life of Jesus before his arrest in the Garden of Gethsemane and his passive acceptance of circumstances afterwards. After his arrest, he kept largely silent - something he had not done previously.

I'm not religious, but I know he constantly challenged the authorities.

Indeed. But after his arrest, his behaviour changed; a spirit of acceptance pervaded his every move.

So what was that about?

Implicit, if not explicit, was an affirmation of uselessness; an acceptance and befriending of holy futility as his circumstances altered. Vanstone was highlighting the fact that sometimes there can be great nobility in waiting and inaction.

There was nothing Jesus could usefully do and that was all right?

Exactly.

And that helps you?

I find it helpful, yes. If we ever link our value and place in the world with being useful, I suspect we become a danger to ourselves and others. Our actions cease to be for others. They become part of our compulsive behaviour, our mechanical behaviour, something we need to do for our self-esteem. Our actions arise out of a sense of deficiency in us which is neither helpful nor happy.

*

One of my sweetest memories is of an old man at the end of summer.

Who was he?

In his youth, he'd been active and applauded. He had created much in the eyes of the world.

But now?

Now things had changed. He pottered about his allotment, un-pressed by time, happy to rake one or two leaves from his borders and ponder the weakening summer sun.

Happy to be useless.

And the contentment in his uselessness shone as bright as anything achieved in his life.

And probably made him peaceful company.

It did, yes.

And so you're better now?

I am thank you but there's something about my illness I don't want to leave behind.

What's that?

The liberating truth of my uselessness.

50. Integrity

Do I have integrity?

So what is integrity?

The English word *integrity* comes from the Latin, *integer* meaning *whole or complete.*

But it's a hard word to define, isn't it? I mean, when we say someone has integrity, what do we really mean?

For me, it's about honesty and truthfulness in our actions, arising from self-knowledge. People are said to have integrity to the extent they act according to their values and principles. They are those with an attractive internal consistency.

That makes sense.

This is why Albert Camus felt able to say: 'Integrity has no need of rules.'

Integrity is its own rule.

I remember once writing the hopeful line: 'One day we'll have hearts and not rules.' It was a hope based on this same idea. Healthy people do not need rules.

Do you?

*

So what is the opposite of integrity? Opposites often help me to understand a word.

The opposite of integrity must be hypocrisy, which is people saying one thing but doing another. Perhaps they condemn something while doing it themselves. They are internally inconsistent and therefore dishonest.

Do as I say, not as I do.

Hypocrisy is the sign of a scattered soul, a desperate soul which grabs at one thing and then another – anything to survive, anything to make them feel better.

So again it's arising from deficiency in us?

Yes and it's not pretty. Hypocrisy is psychological laziness pretending to be good.

So how does solitude help move us nearer integrity?

Like a careful gardener, in solitude we nurture this most substantial of virtues. It's in the soil of honest self-observation that character is formed and we become more substantial people.

How?

We can start by daily noticing the hypocrite in us. Reflect back on your behaviour today. Did you ever condemn others for something you do?

That's quite hard. I mean, facing up to that.

Maybe so but it's also liberating. You have nothing to lose but your claims!

I like that.

Once we calm the need to fool ourselves, we no longer feel the need to fool others which is like fresh air in a prison cell. We sense the difference and they sense the difference.

*

What else do we have to do?

Not a great deal. Once the hypocrite in us is gone, we are naturally people of integrity.

Really?

Yes. With hypocrisy acknowledged, we discover within us a character or substance which has no need of pretence.

As I say, in your heart you are a person of integrity and the most substantial of people. The hypocrite in you keeps you from that truth.

*

Are there any famous role models?

Perhaps no philosopher has had more influence down the centuries than Socrates. And he was the first person to teach the priority of personal integrity.

How did he use the word?

He understood integrity to be a person's duty to themselves rather than to the conventions of the day or the gods of the day or the authorities of the day and the laws they imposed.

That must have got him into trouble.

It did. But it was an approach which has had a profound influence down the ages and a truth which Socrates lived as well as preached.

How?

He was executed for misleading the youth of Athens. In allowing himself to be poisoned by hemlock, the form of execution decreed by law, he showed himself willing to die at the hands of the law rather than give up his right to say what he believed to be true.

Impressive.

He wasn't just another clever teacher putting attention and money above truth. Here was a wholeness, a completeness about his being – as well as courage.

I'm glad you mentioned courage. That seems an important part of integrity.

And other great figures took up the theme. It was Jesus who asked: 'What will a man gain by winning the whole world at the cost of his true self?'

Now there's a question!

While Polonius in Shakespeare's *Hamlet* says: 'This above all: to thine own self be true.'

That's appealing. But what is our true self?

Our true self emerges as we become aware of the unconscious forces that drive us; as we notice and say farewell to our hypocrite. We gradually reclaim a personal integrity which our fear and unknowing has taken from us.

We lean over the fence and say to our fears: 'Can I have my integrity back, please!?'

Something like that.

*

In solitude, we sow the seeds of honesty and truthfulness in our lives and watch the flower of integrity grow.

'Have the courage to say no,' said W. Clement Stone. 'Have the courage to face the truth. Do the right thing because it is right. These are the magic keys to living your life with integrity.'

You could sort through a few of the keys now.

51. Blame

Who am I blaming at present?

She was evacuated from London in 1941 when she was three years old. The bombs were falling on the capital and Georgie and her brother were sent to Hitchin where their aunt and uncle lived. This was good news for Georgie for despite her tender age, she knew she did not like it at home.

So she wasn't sad to be moved?

No, she remembers being happy in Hitchin. She even chose to live there for a few years after the war was over, hoping she would be adopted. But her aunt and uncle were strict.

In what way?

She had to go to church every Sunday, even though the smell of the incence made her feel sick. And if she was naughty or had a tantrum she would be made to sit on the stairs, which were closed off from the front room by a door. This felt very harsh.

I had to sit on the stairs.

If the stairs failed, then it was the garden for Georgie. She had to go down to the bottom of the garden, stand by the shed and 'shake Hitler off her back.'

What?

It's true. Her aunt and uncle would watch from the window as she walked. When she reached the shed she would have to shake herself, as if trying to dislodge a clinging man from her back. With Hitler in the nettles and dealt with, she would then return to the house, her tantrum now subsiding.

*

When Georgie told me the story, the role of Hitler interested me.

Yes, I was wondering about that.

On the Day of Judgement, Adolf Hitler must take responsibility for many things but probably not Georgie's tantrums. Blaming Hitler for these is as ridiculous as Hitler blaming the Jews for Germany's plight in the 1930's.

I was thinking the same.

But of course the human need to blame is far too primal to be concerned with such niceties. Blame is born out of panic and fear. Do not expect it to be reasonable.

So who are you blaming at present?

*

There is short-term relief in blaming someone else.

Yes, but I think it makes us weak.

How?

The opposite of apportioning blame is taking responsibility.

Fair enough.

Taking responsibility is a strong river of energy in us, driving our true self like a river drives a water mill. When we blame someone else, we direct water away from this big river and our true self is enfeebled.

I hadn't really thought of it like that.

If blame is our normal way, the strong river is gradually reduced to a weak river with no energy to drive life, virtue or true action.

And what sort of people can take responsibility?

Taking responsibility is the act of the fearless; blaming others is the act of the frightened and there's no good energy there.

*

So what makes a blamer? I mean I know we all do it, but in some it's a particular poison.

If our parents were always blaming someone else, then it's probable we are today, because blame is a contagious trait. If they were always blaming the government or the immigrants or Mrs Jones at No.4 or us, then probably we too are playing the blame game, looking anywhere but at ourselves.

A lesson we learned without even realising it.

And if we grew up in a climate of blame, in which we felt blamed, this will have been particularly damaging: 'Oh, why did I bring you into the world?' or, 'You're always doing the wrong thing, aren't you?' If we have felt the blame of parents, we will be mustard-keen keen to pass it on to others.

Like Hitler?

Yes, Hitler's father was a brute who beat him and blamed him for everything. And so blame was important for Hitler and became something deluded and repulsive inside him.

But he wasn't to blame for Georgie's tantrums?

No. It's significant that in this true story, she did not want to go back home after the war; that she would have preferred adoption because 'home wasn't a nice place.'

That's quite a sense for a three-year old to have.

It is. And when finally she had to go home, aged 11, she hated it and contracted TB. Her body was perhaps being more honest about her feelings than she was allowed to be.

And the body never lies?

The evidence suggests Georgie's home had much to answer for. But instead of her home, it was Hitler who was blamed for the little girl's troubles.

*

Let's finish by going back 2000 years.

Where to?

We travel to the troubled land of Palestine.

To what end?

I hope it'll be worth it. Something unusual happened.

I can expect to be surprised?

Maybe. The background is this: amid all the power struggles and unrest, the healer and teacher Jesus was thought to be a dangerous figure and was duly executed.

Crucified, like many others, yes, I know.

But here's something to interest us: when hanging on the cross, Jesus did not divert the river of life in him by playing the blame game.

How do you mean?

Speaking of those who had organized this judicial murder and with the nails ripping his flesh, he cried out: 'Forgive them father, they do not know what they are doing.'

An odd thing to say. His accusers knew exactly what they were doing.

But instead of blaming them for their choices, Jesus takes responsibility for his choices. He had continued to confront the religious authorities even when he knew the net was closing around him. That was his choice, and he was taking responsibility for it.

I agree - that is an unusual attitude.

And a refreshing one. It reminded me of a poem by the Sufi Hafiz:

'Blame
Keeps the sad game going.
It keeps stealing all your wealth –
Giving it to an imbecile with no financial skills.

Dear One,
Wise up.'

52. The river within

Is there something beautiful you've hidden?

There is much action in my local park at present: an underground river has been discovered.

How so?

A grant for the park has made a face-lift possible and a survey revealed an underground river which is now much talked of.

So how is it hidden?

Well, while it's called an underground river, this is not strictly true. It's a river that at some point in the past was encased in a concrete tunnel.

Why?

I don't know. Presumably the water was reckoned inconvenient at the time. So for years, we've walked over it, little knowing what was beneath our feet.

But now awareness has broken out in the park!

True. The concrete casing that has held the dark water is being smashed; and there, suddenly close, is a big river seeing the light of day at last.

And about time to.

It was a marvellous if frightening sight when I first saw it. It was a bit like seeing a tiger freed from its cage. Soon the river will be completely revealed and allowed to flow in the open air as once it did in years past.

*

Presumably there's a point to this touching local news?

As I watch the river story unfold - and there's still some way to go – it's hard not to feel the excitement. Equally, it's difficult not to think of the big river within each of us which we have concreted over and made invisible.

How do you mean?

Like my park, we too once had a river flowing through our lives. It was the river of our truest self, our substantial self. But for reasons that were compelling at the time, we buried it and covered it over. And down the years, we've walked over it like there was nothing there.

Is this concrete what they call 'living in denial'?

It is, yes and few write better than Alice Miller about this routine process in humans.

I know the joke about denial not being a river in Egypt.

You and the rest of the world but beyond the comedy is a deep sadness. In *The body never lies* Miller chronicles the effects on the body of our self-deception.

'Ultimately the body will rebel,' she says.

You mean, if we live in significant denial of something, our body will complain?

That's right. 'Even if the body can temporarily be pacified with the help of drugs, cigarettes or medicine,' she continues, 'it usually has the last word because it is quicker to see through self-deception than the mind.'

The body is quicker to see through self-deception than our mind? I'd never have thought that.

It's not so surprising. It was our mind that put our self-deception in place. It's hardly going to assist in its exposure.

I suppose not.

'We may ignore or deride the messages of the body,' continues Miller, 'but its rebellion demands to be heeded because its language is the authentic expression of our true selves and of the strength of our vitality.'

So the question is: does your body speak? And if it does, what does it say and do you take any notice?

*

As I reflect on this, I have one simple question: who lives in denial?

We all do.

I don't.

No one believes they do.

Oh.

Everyone believes denial is a problem for others but not or themselves. They are all-seeing; it's just everyone else who covers their eyes. It's one of self-deception's craftiest tactics.

So our denial has made itself invisible and therefore impregnable! How has it managed this?

We all had our reasons for encasing our river in concrete and sometimes they were very good reasons.

An example?

It's known, for instance, that depression is a particular issue for those who were sexually abused when young. And it's a depression which is difficult to cure because it was necessary for the child to bury their true feelings very deep.

That makes bleak sense.

To be abused by one supposed to be caring for you is a savage experience for the tiny human; and made worse in the long term because we had those feelings when we were still forming as people. This ensured the denial is the toughest concrete to crack.

OK.

There is much in all of us that does not wish to recover our story; and the worse the story, the greater the resistance.

The concrete is hiding things we'd prefer not to see; encasing feelings we'd prefer not to feel.

Indeed. But when the time is right, it's good to begin dismantling the concrete casing and removing it bit by bit from the scene.

It has no place in my local park and it has no place in you. One slab at a time, we work as we are able.

It's time the river saw the sky again.

53. Mindfulness

What is it and how might I use it?

This final chapter is a summary of much of what has gone before and is a distillation of various newspaper pieces I did when my book 'One-Minute Mindfulness' appeared on the shelves:

'Ordinary human unhappiness' was Freud's description of the best possible outcome of psychoanalysis. But where psychoanalysis ends, mindfulness begins. Long practiced in the East, mindfulness is now well established in the West and widely used by those seeking psychological or spiritual change in their lives.

But what is mindfulness and how might we use it? Here are nine nuggets.

*

Seize this moment

Mindfulness is concerned with the present; with keeping your consciousness alive to the present moment. This may appear a simple task but is harder than it sounds. For most of the time, our minds are either taking us back into the past or somewhere into the imaginary future.

To help us to engage with the present moment, our breathing is a great help, because unlike our mind, it's always present. So becoming aware of your breathing now, in and out, in and out, is a wonderful start to becoming present.

The past is stale bread, the future's no bread and the present is fresh bread. The choice is yours.

Notice what is now

We're also helped into the present by noticing things. If we are turning a key in a lock, we notice we are turning a key in a lock. If we are walking down the street, we notice the shifting cloud formations or the negative feelings arising in us towards a car driver. It's about noticing what's happening now.

When we make a cup of tea or do the washing up without thinking 'What am I going to do next?' then we are mindful.

We are happier when we notice the present and let the future take care of itself.

Become the explorer

Mindfulness makes explorers of us; and like all explorers we will need courage if we wish to discover new lands.

 Mindfulness asks us a hard question: are you willing to experience openly what makes you unhappy? We tend to shy away from this because the thought of it makes us scared. And of course this fear is why we became unhappy in the first place. It was because we were scared that we constructed various walls in order to survive.

But if as adults we're willing to face uncomfortable things, then like explorers of old, we'll discover a fresh knowing, virgin territory which restores happiness.

If we're not prepared for such things, then sadly, we'll continue to walk the same mental circles we've always walked.

There is great courage in mindfulness but also great hope. As Julian of Norwich says, 'God did not say 'You shall not be tempest-tossed, you shall not be work-weary, you shall not be discomforted.' But he did say 'You shall not be overcome.'

Nothing can overcome the present.

Stop thinking

Surprisingly, mindfulness encourages us to stop taking our thoughts too seriously. In mindfulness, we say goodbye to the mind.

Mindfulness invites us to stop wandering off into thoughts about the past or about what we want or don't want in the future. Instead, we stop thinking and focus on our breathing and the space that develops inside. We're quiet, present and watch our thoughts as they arise in the space. We don't identify with them; we just watch them.

Soon, we become aware of the restlessness and changeableness of our minds, and in time, we begin take our thoughts less seriously.

This is liberating, as we have been their unquestioning slave for too long. Our thoughts do not offer us the reality we imagine.

Don't censor yourself. Accept yourself

As you experience your breathing, thoughts will arise in you, unbidden. Don't censor them, whatever their nature, but rather allow them all. In accepting them, you accept yourself. As Carl Jung said, 'Enlightenment is not imagining figures of light, but making the darkness conscious.'

If you censor emotions as they appear, they'll bury themselves even deeper within you and you'll never discover anything you didn't know already.

If you allow everything, it may well be that you meet what is making you unhappy, but this is good. How can you say 'goodbye' to it until you've said 'hello'?

Question the negative

We are shaped by what we do with our negative experiences. Depression, for instance, is a turning away from experience in order to avoid emotional pain. Mindfulness doesn't stop negative thoughts or feelings, but does help us to question their believability. Are these negative feelings quite as solid as they appear?

They say painting the front room is all in the preparation; but life is all in the perception, how we perceive events. Mindfulness practice creates in us a sense of water flowing, things passing through, rather than hard blocks of ice inside us, solid and immovable.

Give up your opinions

You cannot be mindful whilst holding onto your opinions. That's like trying to keep dry by jumping into the sea. Your opinions are of no consequence.

Protect the space

Add a table spoon of salt to a glass of water and it makes a significant difference. Add the same spoon of salt to a jug of water and it makes some difference to the taste. Add it to a lake, however, and it hardly affects anything.

Mindfulness makes us larger containers. This happens as we remove from ourselves all the clutter of past and future concerns. In the present, we have endless inner space, which is a great step towards happiness.

Difficult emotions, like salt, may remain but their power to affect us is diffused. Previously they could ruin our day but now they can barely ruin five minutes.

Judge by results

Our judgements of others arise in direct proportion to our self-judgement. As we allow ourselves to notice self-judgement, we also allow ourselves to be free of it and so free others.

People at peace are those who see and accept the truth of who they are, rather than avoiding it and blaming someone else. Such people are less likely to find fault with others and they'll also find barriers of separateness melting.

Mini-biographies
of those quoted

St Anthony 251 – 356

The Egyptian Anthony, born into a wealthy family, was a leading figure in the development of desert monasticism. Lived as a hermit for 13 years where the devil fought him with boredom, laziness and the phantoms of women.

Karen Armstrong b. 1944

A British author, she was originally a Roman Catholic nun who has since moved into a more liberal understanding of her faith. Her writings have sought the common themes shared by different religions, found particularly in the virtue of compassion.

Sir Francis Bacon 1561 – 1626

English philosopher, statesman, scientist, lawyer and author. He knew high office, money troubles and political disgrace. But he was also a forerunner in the methodology of scientific investigation.

Ambrose Bierce 1842 – 1913

An American journalist, short story writer and satirist whose motto in life was 'Nothing matters'. His bleak view of human nature earned him the title 'Bitter Bierce'.

Dietrich Bonhoeffer 1906 - 1945

German pastor, theologian and martyr. Involved in the conspiracy to assassinate Hitler he was arrested in 1943 and executed two years later. He believed there were two guides in life: The needs of one's neighbour and the model of Jesus of Nazareth.

Lord Byron 1788 – 1824

A British poet and aristocrat, he is remembered also for his excessive life of huge debt, numerous love affiars and self-imposed exile in Italy. He died fighting for the Greeks against the Ottoman Empire.

Sister Wendy Beckett b.1930

First Class degree in English Literature from Oxford and famous art critic she now lives a contemplative life in a caravan in the grounds of a Carmelite monastery. She dedicates her life to solitude and prayer but allows herself two hours of work per day.

Buddha 563 – 483 BC

Spiritual teacher from ancient India, now Nepal, who founded Buddhism. Buddha means 'the awakened one' or 'enlightened one'. The world's first self-scientist, who started from the given of human suffering.

Julia Cameron b. 1948

Teacher, author, film maker and journalist perhaps most famous for her best-selling book *The Artist's Way*. After drug and alcohol dependency she discovered creativity as a spiritual path.

Albert Camus 1913 - 1960

French novelist, essayist and playwright. Won the Nobel prize for literature in 1957 for his writings against capital punishment and once played in goal for his university team in Algeria. He died in a car crash.

Oliver Cromwell 1599 – 1658

English military and political leader responsible for the defeat of Charles 1st in the Civil War and for his execution. Ruled England as Lord Protector. Famously asked his portrait artist to paint him 'warts and all.'

Dalai Lama b.1935

Both head of state and spiritual leader of Tibet, he has lived in exile in India since the failed 1959 Tibetan uprising. The title corresponds to that of 'guru'. He is considered to be a manifestation of the bodhisattva of Compassion.

Isak Dinesen 1885 - 1962

Danish aristocrat and writer who spent 24 years running a coffee plantation in Kenya. The film *Out of Africa'* was based on her memoirs.

Meister Eckhart 1260 – 1327

Born in Germany, member of the Dominican Order. Theologian, philosopher and pastor, he was hounded by the Inquisition and tried by the Pope for heresy. His spiritual writings have shone ever brighter down the centuries.

T.S.Eliot 1888 – 1965

Playwright, publisher, literary critic and daring innovator in poetry. His poetry is difficult but he won the Nobel prize for literature in 1948. Born in the USA he became a Bristish citizen in 1927 and his growing sense of God led him to join the Anglican church in the same year.

Epictetus 55 - 135

Born a slave but became a Greek sage and Stoic philosopher. He believed life was determined by fate and beyond our control. We can only accept what happens calmly. Suffering arises from trying to control the uncontrollable.

Lady Gaga b. 1986

Born in New York with Italian ancestry, she was educated in a Roman Catholic convent. She is now a successful pop star and fashion icon, as famous for her outrageous outfits as her music. Also a keen gay rights campaigner.

Gilbert Proesch b. 1943 and George Passmore b.1942

Two artists who collaborate on graphic-style photo-based art work. They claim to be married and live in East London. According to George, 'Nothing happens in the world that does not happen in the East End.'

Joel S. Goldsmith 1892 – 1964

Born in New York, teacher, spiritual healer, mystic and founder of the *Infinite Way* movement, which is also the title of his most famous work.

Antony Gormley b. 1950

Sculptor and Turner Prize winner in 1994. Sees his work, including *The Angel of the North*, as 'an attempt to materialise the place at the other side of appearance where we all live.'

G.I. Gurdjieff 1866 – 1949

An Armenian who was a leading teacher of the '4th Way' and esoteric Christianity. Formed various schools to teach his inner work. 'Life is only real when I am,' one of his books, sums up his teaching on human consciousness.

Hafiz 1325 - 1390

Persian poet who remains the most popular poet amongst Iranians who learn his poems by heart. Born in Shiraz and buried in Shiraz, he combines acute psychology with hope and a delight in God, the beloved.

Dag Hammerskold 1905 – 1961

Swedish diplomat, economist and author he is the only man to receive a postumous Nobel peace prize. Secretary-General of the United Nations, President JK Kennedy called him 'the greatest statesman of our century.'

Thich Nhat Hanh b. 1926

Vietnamese Buddhist monk, teacher, author and peace activist who lives in Plum Village in France, after being exiled from his homeland. International speaker and key figure in bringing the practice of mindfulness to the West.

Herman Hesse 1877 - 1962

German poet and novelist. Son of pietist missionary parents, he explored the relationship between body and mind, winning the Nobel prize for literature in 1946. Perhaps most famous for *Siddharta* and *The Glass Bead Game*.

Peter Hoeg b. 1957

An intenationally-acclaimed Danish novelist, who uses different literary styles and has also spent time as a sailor, ballet dancer and actor.

Cardinal Basil Hume 1923 – 1999

Roman Catholic Archbishop of Westminster who said 'My head is progressive, my heart is conservative.' His motto was that everyone he met was superior to him in some way, which meant everyone he met felt important.

Aldous Huxley 1894 – 1963

English writer from a gifted family, most famous for his novel *Brave New World*. Humanist and pacifist with interest in parapsychology; he advocated the use of mind-altering drugs.

Oliver Wendell Holmes 1841 - 1935

American lawyer and respected and long-serving Associate Jurist of the Supreme Court of the United States. He retired at the age of 90.

Richard Hooker 1554 – 1600

Anglican priest and influential theologian. With his emphasis on scripture, reason and tradition, he is regarded by many as the founder of modern Anglicanism. Unhappily married, but had six children and is buried in Bishopsbourne church in Kent, where there is a statue of him.

Jesus 1 – 33AD

Teacher, prophet, healer in 1st century Palestine crucified for threatening the position of the Temple in Jerusalem and disturbing the status quo. One of the most influential figures in world history, he wrote nothing but his followers claim he rose from the dead.

Julian of Norwich 1342 – 1416

An English mystic, she was an anchoress in Norwich most famous for her 'Revelations of Divine Love'. The first book written by a woman in English it described a series of visions given to her when ill. 'All shall be well, and all shall be well and all manner of things shall be well' are prehaps her most famous words.

Franz Kafka 1883 – 1924

Jewish Czech-born writer considered to be one of the most influential of the 20th century. 'Kafkaesque' has become a word in its own right describing a surreal distortion often with a sense of impending danger.

Rev. Fr. Lambros Kamerides

Born in Constantinople, raised in Athens and educated in Canada where he is now a priest with the Greek Orthodox Church.

Immanuel Kant 1724 – 1804

Influential German philosopher most famous for his *Critique of pure reason*. He said: 'Act that your principle of action might safely be made a law for the whole world.'

Martin Laird

American Roman Catholic, university professor, retreat leader and author of *Into the Silent land*, his popular handbook for those seeking the contemplative way.

Abraham Lincoln 1809 – 1865

With an astute understanding of power, led the USA through the Civil War, preserved the Union and abolished slavery. His Gettysburg Address is the most quoted speech in American history. He was the first US President to be assassinated.

Ann Morrow Lindburgh 1906 - 2001

Pioneering American aviator, author and wife of Charles Lindburgh. A tragic, controversial and inspirational life lived in the public gaze after the kidnap and murder of her first son Charles when 20 months old.

Thomas Merton 1915 – 1968

Trappist monk, poet, social activist and pioneer of dialogue with eastern religions including conversation with the Dalai Lama and Thich Nhat Hahn. His best-selling autobiography *The Seven Storey Mountain* drew many to the monastic life.

Alice Miller 1923 – 2010

Psychologist and author, noted for her books on child abuse. She believed abusive parenting was the cause of the majority of neuroses and psychoses in adults. Critical of psychoanalysis believing it hid rather than revealed the truth.

Henri Nouwen 1932 – 1996

A Dutch priest who taught in various US universities before working with mentally-challenged adults in a L'Arche community in Canada. A prolific spiritual writer, popular across the Catholic and Protestant spectrum.

Mirabel Osler

An English writer perhaps most famous for her book *A gentle plea for chaos* based on her experiences in her garden in Shropshire.

Blaise Pascal 1623 – 1662

Brilliant mathematician, physicist and inventor before a mystical experience in 1654 led him to abandon his scientific work for philosophy and theology. He suffered poor health from the age of 18 and died aged 39.

Plato 427 – 347 BCE

Plato is one of the world's best known and most widely read and studied philosophers. Living in Ancient Greece, he was the student of Socrates and the teacher of Aristotle.

Thomas de Quincey 1785 - 1859

A writer who ran away from his family when young and who knew poor health and constant debt throughout his life. Best known for his 'Confessions of an English opium-eater.' Only three of his eight children survived him.

Rainer Maria Rilke 1875 – 1926

Bohemian-Austrian poet whose poems echo the spirit of the times: the loss of religious belief and profound anxiety. He met Leo Tolstoy in Russia and was close friends with followers of Freud.

Walter Russell 1871 – 1963

American painter, builder and philosopher. He was called 'the Leonado da Vinci of his time' by news anchorman Walter Cronkite. He believed mediocrity is self-inflicted and genius self-bestowed.

Rumi 1207 - 1273

Poet, jurist, theologian and Sufi mystic. Born in what is today Afghanistan and lived and died in what is today Turkey. In 2007 he was declared 'the most popular poet in America'.

Jean-Paul Sartre 1905 - 1980

Leading figure in 20th century French philosophy and literary and philosophical existentialism. Awarded Nobel prize for literature but refused it. Called Che Guevara 'the era's most perfect man.'

Freidrich Schiller 1759 - 1805

A German poet, philosopher and playwright. He was friends with Goethe, was briefly arrested for a pro-republican play, became a professor and died of tuberulosis. Maybe he never recovered from his stern education.

Shakespeare 1564 - 1616

Poet and playwright, widely regarded as greatest writer in English language, though Leo Tolstoy found him repulsive and tedious. Married Ann Hathaway when 18 and had three children but personal details of his life are few.

Angelus Silesius 1624 – 1677

Son of a Polish noble and court physician to an Emperor, he was a poet and mystic. Spoke of the oneness of God and Man: 'I am like God and God like me. I am as large as God. He is as small as I.'

Socrates 469BC – 399BC

Greek philosopher known to us through the writings of his students Plato and Xenophon. His concern for justice and goodness in Athens and his opposition to 'might is right' politics may well have been the reason for his execution.

Chief Standing Bear 1834 – 1908

Native American chief who famously argued in the US court that native Americans are 'persons within the meaning of the law.' As he said, 'The blood is the same colour as yours. God made me, I am a man.'

W. Clement Stone 1902 – 2002

Businessman, philanthropist and self-help author, Stone emphasized using 'a positive mental attitude' to succeed. He once said, 'All I want to do is change the world.'

Publilius Syrus 1st Century BC

Syrian slave educated and freed by his Italian master to become a popular entertainer using mime and improvisation. He was also a writer of pithy sayings.

Mother Syncletica 4th Century AD

A 'desert mother' of the 4th century from a wealthy background and reputedly very beautiful. Her sayings are recorded with those of the desert fathers and she is remembered by the church on January 5th. She died aged 80 in around 350AD.

Laurence Sterne 1713 - 1768

Anglican clergyman and novelist. He only discovered he could write at the age of 46 when he published *The Life and Opinions of Tristram Shandy* to much acclaim. He enjoyed the fame but suffered always with consumption.

Anthony Storr 1920 - 2001

English psychiatrist, inspiring lecturer and author and no stranger to suffering, allegedly prone to the bouts of depression endured by his mother. Married twice, with three daughters, his first marriage ending in divorce. Son of a clergyman and asthma sufferer when young. Had piano lesson the day of his death.

Thomas Szasz b.1920

Hungarian-born psychiatrist who emigrated to the US in 1938. Strong opponent of of medical professionals who claim control over people's lives; refutes the 'fact' of mental inllness. The American Humanist Association named him Humanist of the Year in 1973.

Rabindranath Tagore 1861 – 1941

Bengali poet, novelist, musician, painter and playwright. The first non-European to be awarded the Nobel prize for literature, he wrote the national anthems for both India and Bangladesh.

Paul Tillich 1886 – 1965

German-American theologian and philosopher who moved to the US in 1933 after clashing with the new Nazi regime. He once said 'Astonishment is the root of philosophy.'

Mother Teresa 1910 – 1997

Catholic nun from Albania who founded the Missionaries of Christ in Calcutta in 1950. She won the Nobel peace prize but also knew long periods of depression and despair during which she 'felt no presence of God whatsoever.'

Steve Turner

English music journalist, biographer of Cliff Richard and others and popular poet. His first book for children *The day I fell down the toilet* sold over 120,000 copies. He lives in London.

Desmond Tutu b. 1931

Retired Archbishop in South Africa and key figure in the country's struggle against apartheid. Influenced by white Bishop Trevor Huddleston but called 'evil' by Zimbabwean leader Robert Mugabe. Still a strong voice on the world stage.

Chuang Tzu

Lived in 4th or 3rd century BC. A minor government official in China, he believed the processes of nature unified all things so people should live at one with nature, not impose upon it. He believed one could do more by doing nothing.

W.H. Vanstone 1923 – 1999

Intellectually gifted Anglican priest ripe for a glittering academic career. Instead, he devoted his life to parish ministry on housing estates and writing books including his classic, *Love's endeavour, love's expense.*

William Wordsworth 1770 – 1850

English Romantic poet who lived in the Lake District. Famously 'wandered lonely as a cloud' but friends with the poet Coleridge and married with 5 children. He had another child from a liaison in Paris before the revolution.

Virginia Woolf 1882 – 1941

English author, essayist and publisher, she suffered mental health problems throughout her life after being sexually abused by her half-brothers. Wrote prolifically and ground-breakingly but committed suicide in the River Ouse in Sussex.

Robert W. Woodruff 1869 - 1985

President of the Coca-Cola Company from 1923 – 1954 during which time it became an international business. Used his fortune to help educational causes, though when at university himself, he excelled at 'cutting classes and spending money.'

Paperbacks also available from
White Crow Books

Leo Tolstoy—*My Religion:
What I Believe*
ISBN 978-1-907355-23-3

Leo Tolstoy—*On Life*
ISBN 978-1-907355-91-2

Leo Tolstoy—*Twenty-three Tales*
ISBN 978-1-907355-29-5

Leo Tolstoy—*What is Religion
and other writings*
ISBN 978-1-907355-28-8

Leo Tolstoy—*Work While
Ye Have the Light*
ISBN 978-1-907355-26-4

Leo Tolstoy with Simon Parke—
Conversations with Tolstoy
ISBN 978-1-907355-25-7

Vincent Van Gogh with
Simon Parke—*Conversations
with Van Gogh*
ISBN 978-1-907355-95-0

Howard Williams with an
Introduction by Leo Tolstoy—*The
Ethics of Diet: An Anthology of
Vegetarian Thought*
ISBN 978-1-907355-21-9

Allan Kardec—*The Spirits Book*
ISBN 978-1-907355-98-1

Wolfgang Amadeus Mozart
with Simon Parke—
Conversations with Mozart
ISBN 978-1-907661-38-9

Jesus of Nazareth with
Simon Parke—*Conversations
with Jesus of Nazareth*
ISBN 978-1-907661-41-9

Thomas à Kempis with Simon
Parke—*The Imitation of Christ*
ISBN 978-1-907661-58-7

Emanuel Swedenborg—
Heaven and Hell
ISBN 978-1-907661-55-6

P.D. Ouspensky—*Tertium Organum:
The Third Canon of Thought*
ISBN 978-1-907661-47-1

Dwight Goddard—*A Buddhist Bible*
ISBN 978-1-907661-44-0

Leo Tolstoy—*The Death
of Ivan Ilyich*
ISBN 978-1-907661-10-5

Leo Tolstoy—*Resurrection*
ISBN 978-1-907661-09-9

Michael Tymn—*The Afterlife
Revealed*
ISBN 978-1-970661-90-7

Guy L. Playfair—*If This Be Magic*
ISBN 978-1-907661-84-6

Julian of Norwich with
Simon Parke—*Revelations of
Divine Love*
ISBN 978-1-907661-88-4

Maurice Nicoll—*The New Man*
ISBN 978-1-907661-86-0

Carl Wickland, M.D.—*Thirty Years
Among the Dead*
ISBN 978-1-907661-72-3

Allan Kardec—*The Book on
Mediums*
ISBN 978-1-907661-75-4

John F. Mack—*Passport to the
Cosmos*
ISBN 978-1-907661-81-5

**All titles available as eBooks, and selected titles available in Hardback and
Audiobook formats from www.whitecrowbooks.com**

Lightning Source UK Ltd.
Milton Keynes UK
UKOW052254050912

198521UK00001B/124/P